What People Are Saying for...

The 7 Power Words: A Guide to a Truly Happy and Meaningful Life

I have been a psychologist in my private practice in Australia for the past nine years. I have counseled hundreds of individuals from diverse demographics—age, ethnicity, religion, etc. I have taught and mentored individuals to develop confidence and positive attitudes for many years.

I have read and recommended several self-help books to assist with bringing positive changes to the lives of different individuals. I believe in the saying: "You are defined by the people you are with and the books you read."

After reading *The 7 Power Words: A Guide to a Truly Happy and Meaningful Life"* by Letty R. Vendramini, I realized here is a book that could equip anyone with a summary of the most inspiring verses, great wisdom, and workable strategies from famous philosophers, religious leaders, and best-selling authors. It will be the self-help book I recommend to my clients and patients, and of course my friends, family, and colleagues.

Letty is one lady who truly understands our modern society with its many social pressures. I have witnessed her authentic compassion, and how she can bring comfort even in her business relationships.

The 7 Power Words... will help you to move forward to new levels of well-being, success, and happiness in ALL areas of your life. A must read!

Madonna Abella

Psychologist, Project Leader, Businesswoman

This book is a source of vital information and insights—very helpful, honest, and trustworthy. Letty's great style of writing is refreshing and informative. The pieces of advice, powerful messages, helpful tips, and step-by-step strategies are among the best you can read towards achieving a fulfilling, joyful, and happy life. Now is Your chance and opportunity to grab a copy of this awesome book.

Ewen Chia

Internet Marketing Guru, Singapore

EwenChia.com

Outstanding! Without a doubt one of the best books on Personal Development out there today!

Belinda Rituper

Nurse, Mater Brisbane Hospital, Australia

PROLIFIC!
A great literary and spiritual reading!
DYNAMITE!

The words, messages, and teachings of this book are

dynamite because the author is the

EPITOME of each of these powerful teachings. She

lives them, she is each message! I say this because I

know the author. We ate from the same plate, drank from the same

glass, sang the same songs, laughed together, held hands as we climbed

the same hills

and mountains,

dreaming big dreams, reaching for the stars ...

YES, I KNOW THIS AUTHOR: SHE HAPPENS TO

BE MY SISTER.

BUY THIS BOOK,

carry it with you as your second bible, or as classic

masterpiece everywhere you go; or—give it as a gift. It

can be someone else's

resurrection when his or her soul has turned to ashes.

CARMENCITA R. BRIONES, M.A.

WHO'S WHO AMONG AMERICA'S TEACHERS

PROFESSOR, LOS ANGELES COMMUNITY COLLEGES,

CALIFORNIA, USA

Hi Letty,

The last year for me has been the most traumatic ever in my life.

Two bouts of cancer and a major brain seizure have left me disabled,

disheartened, and I suppose, depressed. The two major operations and the

long months in bed were horrific for an active person such as myself.

Life was at a very low point for me.

A few months ago, I joined your mailing list and also read your latest book—*The 7 Power Words: A Guide to a Truly Happy and Meaningful Life.* This has given me such a profound change in my attitude and outlook on life that even I am surprised!

The days are brighter. The smiles are bigger. The future is now okay! Please keep writing.

Best regards,

BILL BATEMAN

WORLD INTERNET PRODUCTS

MANAGER

MELBOURNE, AUSTRALIA

"It takes someone to lead you if you do not act," so the saying goes. Letty's book poses a challenge to all that it is not impossible to eliminate unhappiness and failure by implementing *The 7 Power Words: A Guide to a Truly Happy and Meaningful Life.* This powerful book offers an opportunity of a life-transforming formula that empowers anyone to live a life that matters and find real happiness in his or her life.

JOHN V. CHILDERS

WEALTHACADEMY.COM

Letty Vendramini has created a Masterpiece of Inner Happiness with her latest work, *The 7 Power Words: A Guide to a Truly Happy and Meaningful Life.* She has artfully crafted together a compilation of different works and authors into a distinctive book to which she has added her own feeling and touch. It is an inspiring work and a "must-read" for those that seek inner peace and personal development in an age of caring.

KEN TRIAT

PERSONAL DEVELOPMENT AND COACH

WWW.PHYSICSOFGETTINGWEALTHY.COM

Letty Vendramini is one of the happiest people I've met. In *The 7 Power Words…*, you will discover that happiness is always a viable choice. This book is a compilation of artful and simple and timeless tips to get the best from life no matter what circumstances are present.

DEBORAH TORRES PATEL

MENTOR, COACH, TRAINER, CONSULTANT

WWW.EXPRESSINGYOU.COM

SINGAPORE

The 7 Power Words… is an easy to read book—an affirmation to living life to the fullest. With quotes and wisdom from positive, inspirational authors and from the expertise of Letty Vendramini, it is a "Guide to Better Living."

EVELYN ZARAGOZA

PUBLISHER AND MANAGING EDITOR

THE PHILIPPINE COMMUNITY HERALD NEWSPAPER

SYDNEY, AUSTRALIA

Letty is a person who shows great passion, strong determination, unfailing dedication, and compelling drive in her beliefs and actions.

Letty's new book—*The 7 Power Words: A Guide to a Truly Happy and Meaningful Life*—teaches you how to organize yourself and erase lifelong negative patterns. Her powerful book gives you the ultimate weapon to conquer YOUR unhappiness, fear, and meaninglessness in life. Letty genuinely wants to help. She lives her life with profound passion, and she lives it to the fullest.

Congratulations!

Nik Halik

CEO and Founder

Financial Freedom Institute (FFI)

Melbourne, Australia

Reading Letty Vendramini's book is not only educational; it proved to be the start of an amazing journey of discovery and reflection about myself. Happiness is indeed a voyage, not a destination. The "Fifteen Steps on How to Be Happy" is a helpful revelation that everyone should practice.

Happiness Is Attainable.

Let Us Choose to Be Happy!

Ma. Neria Nidea Soliman, JP

Sydney, Australia

Letty has found the "secret" behind *The Secret*. If there is one piece of information everyone needs, it's something to be happy about☺. This book will definitely give you step-by-step strategies on how to achieve that. Highly recommended!"

Lourders P. Elardo

SpeakingWithLourdes.com

It is indeed a very inspiring book, and the words of wisdom from the passages are truly powerful.

Malyn Chun

President

Filipino Community Council of Australia

There is no question in my mind that Letty's book is timely and compelling, as neither the new generation nor reformation can ultimately change society. Rather, this book is a powerful guide—one so persuasive that it sweeps away the old myths of frustration, boredom, loneliness; and her book is so inclusive that it gathers all the bits of our problems into a coherent whole, one that even shines some lights into someone else's life/future so that he or she can take the next step forward and think that life is "short" and we don't want to waste it; and publishing this book is simply a life saver.

Letty's book is one of the most important books I have read this year. Indeed a remarkable feat of publishing. Well done, Letty!

Imelda Galmesa, JP

Journalist, Federal Public Servant

and Community Leader

Adelaide, South Australia

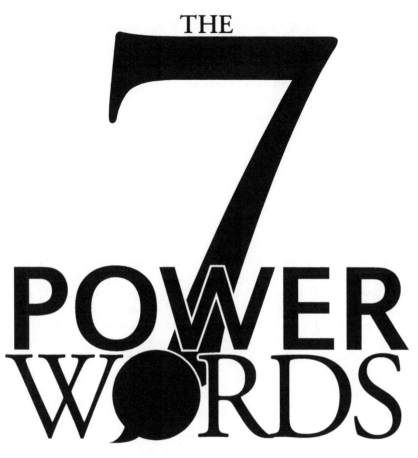

THE 7 POWER WORDS

A GUIDE TO A TRULY HAPPY AND MEANINGFUL LIFE

LETTY R. VENDRAMINI

MORGAN JAMES PUBLISHING • NEW YORK

ISBN: 978-1-60037-544-6 (Paperback)
Library of Congress Control Number: 2008941212

Published by:

MORGAN · JAMES
THE ENTREPRENEURIAL PUBLISHER ™
www.morganjamespublishing.com

Morgan James Publishing, LLC
1225 Franklin Ave Suite 325
Garden City, NY 11530-1693
Toll Free 800-485-4943
www.MorganJamesPublishing.com

Cover/Interior Design by:
Rachel Lopez
rachel@r2cdesign.com

Chapter Photos by:
Franco Giorgio Vendramini
Author Photos by:
Peter Michael Stevens

In an effort to support local communities, raise awareness and funds, Morgan James Publishing donates one percent of all book sales for the life of each book to Habitat for Humanity.
Get involved today, visit
www.HelpHabitatForHumanity.org.

Habitat for Humanity®
Peninsula
Building Partner

We are grateful to Grand Central Publishing and Joel Osteen for permission to reprint excerpts from the book, Your Best Life Now.

Dedication

To anyone seeking or dreaming of living a more empowered, happy, meaningful, and joy-filled existence…

To the future generation, that you might plant seeds today to equip yourself for tomorrow and never have to worry about the future again and that you might invest in yourself now, for the beginning is just the half of it.

To my father, who left this world a happy man and bequeathed to his children his own yardstick of love, service, and generosity toward others, which is the real meaning of happiness.

Living is a responsibility.

Life is searching. Seek with the desire to know more,
and find with the desire to seek more.

Happiness is anywhere
People take the time to care.

To your success, happiness, and a meaningful life!

LETTY RULLODA STEVENS VENDRAMINI

xiii

Contents

Some identify happiness with virtue,

some with practical wisdom, others

with a kind of philosophic wisdom,

others with these or one of these,

accompanied by pleasure.

—Aristotle, *Ethics*

The tragedy of life is what dies inside

a man while he lives.

—Albert Schweitzer

Dream as if you'll live forever. Live as if you'll die today.

—James Dean, singer

Life is either a daring adventure

or nothing.

- HELEN KELLER

The journey of a thousand miles

begins with a single step.

—Lao Tzu, Chinese philosopher

Go confidently in the direction of your Dreams. Live the life you've imagined.

-HENRY DAVID THOREAU (1817-1962)

US ESSAYIST, POET, NATURALIST

Foreword

The power of our words is often underestimated. Both life and death lie in words that we speak. Letty Vendramini has captured the importance of this principle and brought it to life in her book: *The 7 Power Words: A Guide to a Truly and Meaningful Life.* Four of those words could be in a book of their own. Words like Live, Love, Laugh and Learn are so important in everyday life. These truly are powerful words. My favorite book says that if you love your neighbor as yourself, everything else is taken care of. In this book, she gives you step-by-step strategies on how to live your life the way it was meant to be—to live a life of fullness. Life wasn't meant to be wasted and squandered, and after reading this book you will not have any excuse. Letty not only gives you the knowledge but gives you the 'how-tos.' There are two forces that are vital in our happiness: our relationships and our achievements. *The 7 Power Words...* give you the keys to success in both areas. Remember: your past does not equal your future. Letty has been inspired by some of the greatest philosophers we have ever known and has compiled their words of wisdom into this book. She has poured her heart and her soul into the pages of this book. She has shared what has taken many years to learn. It is my heartfelt prayer that this book will inspire and challenge you to find the success that God has in store for you. I'll leave you with this: whatever you say will become your reality. If you say you're stupid, you're stupid. If you say you're smart, you're smart. Whatever you say you are, that's what you are. If you live by powerless words, you will live a powerless life. If you live by words of power, you will have a life filled with power.

Henry Ford said it best: "If you say you can, you can; if you say you can't, you can't. Either way you're still right." *The choice is yours.*

JOHNNY WIMBREY

INTERNATIONAL MOTIVATIONAL SPEAKER

PUBLISHED AUTHOR

TELEVISION TALK SHOW HOST

If one advances confidently in the direction of his dreams, and endeavors to live the life which he has imagined, he will meet with success unexpected in common hours.

—Henry David Thoreau, *Walden*

Preface

At last, you now can discover the seven simple but powerful words that will enable you to live a meaningful, peaceful, and truly happy life from one convenient, inexpensive guidebook!

My professional backgrounds are in the fields of philosophy and English (for my first degree), and social worker–counseling (for my second degree). While teaching, I also took a year of my master's in English literature. My teaching in the tertiary level spans twelve years as an educator and four years as social worker–counselor and private practitioner. People familiar with my writings say I am a prolific writer. I am also a newspaper columnist, reporter, and correspondent; editor, author, and an EzineArticles.com "expert author"; Million Dollar International Speaker alumna, Internet infopreneur, and a personal and happiness coach.

As you probably could tell by my many titles, *I love to live life to the fullest!* Now I want to help you do the same thing. Why? Because "I walk my talk" and definitely achieve the positive outcomes that I desire in my life. Put now into action what your mind conceives and believes, and you will achieve what you ask for!

In the various roles and designations I have undertaken in the recent past in both my professional, social, and personal life, I have met and dealt with a myriad of people from all walks of life, the rich and famous and the poor alike, people of various ethnicities, demographics, age, professions, social status, and religious beliefs, people who experience daily life's challenges, be they career problems, family issues, negative relationships, psychological and physical worries, and social and structural constraints. I have dealt with people's real-life situations and near-death experiences. I have seen the challenging experiences that my clients and many other people in society go through in their daily lives.

If you read our newspapers and watch our news programs and television talk shows, you will realize that there are people who are dissatisfied with their current jobs, people who are dissatisfied with the amount of money they make or how far they have to drive to get to their place of employment, people who experience feelings of depression, stress, lack of productivity, lack of direction, inadequacy, or general feelings of discontent, people who desperately want to add meaning to their lives and relationships but *who don't know how* and try to do it all in the wrong ways, such as buying extravagant things to make themselves feel good, partying, or even doing destructive things to themselves, either purposely or not, without realizing they're on the road to their own destruction!

Why? Because they do not have the knowledge, the skills, or the words they need to communicate their ideas and needs, and because they have not yet found the strategies—the "how-tos"—to implement and improve their life situations, the strategies that will allow them to achieve personal fulfillment, success, joy, inner peace, health, wealth, and a truly meaningful and happy life.

Hence, there are people who "sleepwalk" through life, never really caring about anything, never letting themselves experience true excitement and true enjoyment.

That, in a nutshell, is why I have written this book, *The 7 Power Words: A Guide to a Truly Happy and Meaningful Life:* to provide you with the "owner's manual" that will help you squeeze as much of happiness out of life as possible.

This book is a guide for meaningful and successful living. In it, I reveal the principles that govern life as well as unique insights that you can use to establish your personal life philosophy and fill your life with purpose and meaning, as I have done for myself.

In the process of writing *The 7 Power Words: A Guide to a Truly Happy and Meaningful Life* and integrating my own professional expertise and rich experiences, I find I owe my feats of inspiration to the following:

- The sublime thoughts, the practical wisdom, the deep insights, and helpful strategies that many of our famous philosophers and great thinkers in the history of mankind have handed down from generation to generation, which I learned over the course of the four years in which I earned my philosophy degree.

- Writers, authors, and their outstanding and noble thoughts, ideas, viewpoints, and wisdom about life in general or other areas of their expertise.

- The learned and those skilled in their own creative and strategic ways.

- Successful, wealthy businessmen with unique stories and strategies who made their dramatic rise in life from rags to riches.

- Our driven and astute world leaders of past and present who have strongly guided us in both moments of fame and glory and in moments of shame and dishonor but left vital lessons to learn.

- Our peaceful, calm, and collected spiritual mentors who guide us and show us the right way.

- Noble men and women alike who know how to give of themselves, to serve and love endlessly without counting the cost.

- My family and loved ones with whom I learned my values early in life, such as self-respect, integrity, honor, the need to educate or invest in one's self, loving, giving, sharing, persistence, determination, drive, passion, kindness, forgiveness, and—not to forget—learning how to be happy.

- But above all things, my acknowledgment of a God who is the Prime Mover of this Universe that we all live in, the God that makes all things possible, and the one whose name I want to Glorify for His abundant blessings in my life.

These—and all these people in the world—have in one way or another powerfully contributed to my life and played a positive, pivotal role in catapulting me to where I am today and moving forward for tomorrow.

It is therefore my deep hope and purpose to also share with you my knowledge, wisdom, skills, and understanding about the many complexities of life and to impart strategies for you to know, to learn, and to implement in order to achieve the happiness you're looking for in your life. I'd love to share what I know and give you help unselfishly.

If you currently feel like you are missing something, this comprehensive yet easy-to-follow book will provide you with the secrets of seven simple but powerful words you need to know to replace your sense of aimless dissatisfaction with a sense of purposeful living. The simple truth is, you only get one shot of life, so you may as well give it your best effort and make it enjoyable, meaningful, adventurous, challenging, successful, and as happy as you can.

You see, the life you are managing is your own. The emotional life, the social life, the spiritual life, the physical life—all of it is your own. Manage it in a purposeful way, and you will have what you want. You are your own life strategist. Really, one cannot participate in this mysterious act of living with any hope of satisfaction unless one understands a few rules and life strategies.

The wisdom of the Chinese philosopher Confucius sums up the next crucial step you are going to take in your life. This is what Confucius said: "The journey of a thousand miles begins with the first step."

That's right. Take the first step to learn the secrets of *The 7 Power Words...* and start living the life you have dreamt of—now!

To your success, happiness, and a meaningful life!

LETTY R. VENDRAMINI

Acknowledgments

I want to give due credit and recognition, with deep gratitude to the following:

- John Childers (USA), mentor/trainer/mastermind in our Million Dollar International Speaker Training
- Jennifer Carter (USA), mastermind coach
- Deborah Torres Patel (Singapore), my former one-on-one coach and now my current mentor
- Johnny Wimbrey (USA), published author, motivational speaker, television talk show host and training director of Success University for obliging me with writing the foreword to my book
- Ewen Chia and David Cavanagh, my Internet business marketing gurus, from Singapore and Thailand, respectively
- Nik Halik (Melbourne, Australia), CEO and founder, Financial Freedom Institute, for his great contribution to my testimonials
- My Internet marketer colleagues, friends, clients, customers, and readers who read my book and generously provided me with their powerful testimonials
- Peter Michael Stevens, my twenty-five-year-old son, a special thank-you for his tremendous help in all aspects of the

preparation, production, and final completion of my original self-published book and audiobook, and for his contributions as our Web master, programmer, and graphic designer

- Franco, my ever-supportive husband, whose passion with life and immense enjoyment of nature enables us to discover excitement and beauty that life brings into our lives

- My sister from Los Angeles, California, Carmencita R. Briones, a college professor listed in *Who's Who in America's Teachers,* for her moral support and relevant comments on my book

- William Mark Stevens, my seven-year-old grandson, who is a joy to all and whose childish and hearty laughter, sweet smiles, loving actions, and godly ways inspired me to write more about laughter

- Belinda Rituper, a very dedicated professional nurse and William's mom, whose unique love and commitment, unselfish support, and service to her family is indeed commendable and endearing

- Andreas Bianchi, our enthusiastic and happy friend from Switzerland, and Marco Vendramini, my step-son, for their innately humorous natures and infectious laughter

- Boris Anticevich, our long-time dear friend, who took time and interest to read my book and gave his intelligent insights

- My loving family overseas who I miss, cherish, and love dearly: our role model parents who nurtured us in a loving, giving, caring, peaceful, and happy family; my enthusiastic, optimistic, happy and friendly but now bedridden ninety-four-year-old mother, whose fun-loving ways I took after; my deceased father, to whom I dedicate my book, our family hero and beacon light

- But above all, I thank our ever-loving Father above, who has given to me abundantly in every area of my life—physically, mentally, and spiritually—and who wants me to serve mankind for his greater glory. I believe He has given me a mission on earth to glorify his name—the Creator of the Universe that we all live in today!

- Last but not the least, to Morgan James Publishing for making me a part of their family and who took interest to publish my book, a big thank you!

Thank you and I appreciate you all for your support and interest in this significant endeavor!

Sincerely,

LETTY R. VENDRAMINI

See the world for what it really is.

Introduction

I pose this question to you: who could put a price on a life well lived?

Is your life full and rewarding and everything that you hoped it would be? Or are you dreaming of living a more meaningful life, a life filled with joy and happiness? If so, I have two things to say to you: you are not alone, and you've definitely found the right book for you—*The 7 Power Words*: A *Guide to a Truly Happy and Meaningful Life.*

Here's why:

In less than ten minutes, I am going to reveal how you can have the life of your dreams, a life filled with personal success, inner peace, fulfillment, wealth, health, and real, personal happiness.

What about you? Are you happy? Really happy? Are you satisfied with your current job? Are you satisfied with your current circumstances? Are you satisfied with the relationships you have in your life? Or do you feel like you are missing something? Do you ever feel lost? Have you ever dreamt of leading a more meaningful and powerful life? Do you have other important dreams in your life that you haven't yet fulfilled and want to achieve?

Well, I'm here to tell you that it is *possible* to have the life you've been longing for. That's right, *just seven powerful words* are all that stand between you and your dream life. If you learn these seven words, keep them at the top of your mind, and stay focused on them, your life can quickly be filled with happiness, meaning, and power.

That's why I urge you, if your life is not all that you hoped it would be, if you are not truly happy and your life lacks meaning, to read this book right now, *The 7 Power Words: A Guide to a Truly Happy and Meaningful Life!* It's that important!

In fact, you're about to discover how living by *The 7 Power Words...* can quickly and easily give you the life you've always wanted! I am therefore going to share with you this very interesting, exciting, and engaging topic that I am very passionate about: *life and how to live it to the fullest!* This is a tremendous value and an opportunity to develop the skills you need to live an enjoyable, meaningful life.

You will learn, among other things:

- How to fill your life with real happiness and meaning
- How to live your life to the full
- How to replace a sense of aimless dissatisfaction with a sense of purpose
- Why service is the pathway to significance and where service really starts
- The ultimate goal for life on earth
- The attitude you should have every day of your life
- Why life without this is useless
- The truth behind the statement "everyone you meet is your mirror" and how to use this truth to brighten your life as well as the lives of others you come in contact with

- Where your happiness really comes from—you are sure to be surprised when you read this, for it goes against all our natural instincts!
- LOVE, four letters to live by, plus the easiest way to find love
- How to add laughter to your life, plus why men and women differ in what they think is funny

The 7 Power Words: A Guide to a Truly Happy and Meaningful Life comprises seven chapters and corresponding subtopics.

Chapter 1 is Power Word Number One: "Live!" It presents to you the wisdom of great men and women of past and present as they pass on to you their wisdom, how to use it and take action, and be successful and happy in life. It gives you three strategies on how to manage and value your everyday life and another seven ways on how to live your best life now. Two practical readings highlight the importance of living your everyday life. It includes the right mental attitude, which is vital to living your daily life. You will learn twelve tips on right mental attitude. It also includes Pamela Owens Renfro's words that encourage you to build the power to value your life and continue to live your life and "to be strong and not to give up!"

Chapter 2 covers Power Word Number Two: "Love!" It asks the question: "what is love and how do you develop your ability to love?" There are four factors to consider in love and relationships; communication, honesty, trust and giving. You will learn the four letters of "LOVE" to help you become a more loving person, as well as fifteen words and phrases that you will want to forget and their corresponding words and phrases that you will want to remember.

From the first two power words, "Live" and "Love," you advance to Power Word Number Three: "Think!" Your actions are results of your thoughts. Your thinking can make or unmake your dreams or your goals. You will find these topics: the role of perception and communication in the process of love, the Law of Attraction and how to think rationally, and the power of music and how it can be instrumental in your thinking and life. It explores critical thinking and creative thinking and shows the relevance of "core-level mental triggers" that could enable you to make dreams that you want to achieve.

As we think, we also learn. Thinking and learning go hand in hand in the process of moving forward from thinking to learning. You will learn to make use of opportunities that come your way. If you don't use your opportunities, you will miss out. Just like that! Donald Trump's vision of success by making use of your opportunities is summed up when he said: "90 percent of success begins by just showing up." Use the opportunities that come your way! Your success may not be far away.

Also in chapter 3 are the following topics: learning with purpose, learning from faith and prayer, and learning that wisdom is supreme, as written in the books of all books, the Holy Bible.

"Give!" is Power Word Number Five. Chapter 5 discusses giving as an art and the universal law of giving and receiving and presents four guides to the law of giving. The joy of giving occupies a big portion of the text and teaches you that once you begin to practice giving, it will enhance your happiness. The pleasures of giving are huge! You can begin to enjoy yourself and laugh at the world when you feel you have contributed to the happiness of another person on earth. I also integrate Rick Warren's ideas on using your "SHAPE" when giving.

What is laughter? What makes you laugh? Chapter 6 explores Power Word Number Six: "Laugh!" It examines the nature of laughter and explains the gender differences of laughter, what laughter can do to you, and how the increase of serotonin in your brain brought about by laughing can alleviate depression and other mental problems. Read on!

Finally, Power Word Number Seven: "Be Happy!" That's chapter 7 and the last chapter for you. But what is happiness? Here, I present fifteen steps on how to be happy and seventeen happiness tips you can implement to become happy. There are three warnings about happiness. Take note. It is essential to heed these three warnings. There are five great laws of success and happiness. And how do you apply the ABCs of Happiness in your life? Someone has said that "there is no real excellence in this world which can be separated from right living."

Read this book, *The 7 Power Words: A Guide to a Truly Happy and Meaningful Life,* and then you can begin your right way of living by learning and implementing *The 7 Power Words* that will empower you to achieve your personal success, fulfillment, spirituality, inner peace, wealth, health, and real personal joy and happiness in your life and take your life to the next level.

Don't be the herd. Rise above to the next level of your happiness! Remember:

"Happiness is a choice."

"Choose to be happy!"

To your happiness!

The unexamined life is not worth living.

—Socrates

Power Word Number One:

Live!

Whatever you can do, or dream you can, begin it. Boldness has genius, power, and magic in it. Begin it now.

—Goethe

They say that we have but one life to live, so we might as well live it to our best!

But having said that, we still hear of some unbelievable, eyebrow-raising cases in which "people who have left planet Earth" have miraculously come back to life in unimaginable ways! Scary but true, and it has happened and may still be happening around you or in parts of the world that you don't hear about.

1

Hence, there is all the more reason to think that your life is valuable, so valuable that you should not mess it up or ruin it, not even for just one single day. A day is all you have. Yes, you have only one day to live, every day! Therefore, value each day of your life. There are no first regrets, so they say. Regrets are always final.

LIVE: Words of Wisdom from Great Men and Women Past and Present

Every day is a new day in your life, because you only have one day to live—you have only today! That's why they say, "There is no dress rehearsal in life. This is the real thing." I get this message. Do you? It is therefore imperative that you hone your skills for learning about life—your life—and how to live your life every single day.

I have a habit that I practice daily. Every morning upon arising from bed, I recite the verse from Psalm 118:24: "This is the day the Lord has made; let us rejoice and be glad in it." Moreover, I make it a point to make my day the *best* I possibly can and do the things that I can do just for *today.* And I remind myself that this is the first day of the rest of my life and I only have one life to live.

Therefore, live for this moment, because you do not know what tomorrow brings. You are lucky if you have another new day, for tomorrow may never come. And that's the reality of life on earth. You may be here today and gone tomorrow. If you have to live your dream, you have to wake up and do something about it now, because success is living the moment. Ralph Waldo Emerson, talking about life, said:

The greatest use of life is to spend it for something that will outlast it.

Helen Keller, though blind and deaf, was thinking along remarkably similar lines when she said the following about the importance of life:

Life is either a daring adventure or nothing.

The great Greek philosopher Socrates gives us relevant insight with these classic words of wisdom:

The unexamined life is not worth living.

To get the best in life—success, fulfillment, prosperity, and happiness—you have to examine yourself. Yes, you have to investigate, learn, and implement the strategies that lead towards the goal of happiness in your personal life. As Socrates also said:

To find yourself, think for yourself.

This topic will be further discussed in chapter 3, which is devoted to power word number three: think.

Let me share with you an experience that I will never forget and an insight I learned from the famous playwright William Shakespeare.

I vividly remember the time I was invited to teach summer classes in English literature for secondary students in a private school for girls. Since it was between semesters of my tertiary teaching of philosophy and English subjects at another nearby college, I accepted the offer. On second thought, I took the challenge of the offer because I was in my first year of studies of my master's degree in English literature at the Ateneo University.

One of the course subjects that had been selected that summer was a study of the famous playwright William Shakespeare and his well-known play *As You Like It*. I taught a one-hour class every day on Shakespeare and two additional classes on different subjects. For five weeks, we engaged in interactive sessions about the play, and students informally acted the play out in class in a manner that was interesting and exciting for both the students and myself.

This brief teaching experience made a strong impression on me, as did the thoughts Shakespeare expressed in his play. The most significant thing I took home with me after teaching the course was Shakespeare's use of metaphorical language in the play, which continues to resonate in my brain whenever I talk or listen to conversations about life. In one of the most memorable passages in the play, Shakespeare wrote:

> *All the world is a stage, and all men and women merely players; they have their exits and their entrances; and one man in his time plays many parts.*

This is indeed a powerful thought! As I said earlier, one must live one's life, play one's part, every single day.

Similarly, Voltaire says that each player accepts the cards life deals, but once they are in hand, each alone must decide how to play the cards in order to win the game: and *life* is the game. That is how it happens.

On another note, Eileen Caddy sheds a different light on this: as a player, "you are never asked to do more than you are able without being given the strength and ability to do it." The Bible itself attests to what Eileen said, for it teaches you that the Father above does not give you problems that you cannot handle. However, you should never be afraid to tread the path alone. You should know which is your path and follow it wherever it may lead you; do not feel you have to follow in someone else's footsteps.

It's interesting to note how Albert Schweitzer envisioned the tragedy of man.

The tragedy of life is what dies inside a man while he lives.

Schweitzer's vision compels you to achieve positive things in your life while you are alive and breathing. Take a brave step and make a move to change from inaction to action. Move forward and live!

Mother Teresa herself taught the whole world during her missions to help the poor that if one desires change, "one must be that change before that change can take place." Mother Teresa's wisdom reflected the philosophy of India's leader, Mahatma Gandhi.

It is not impossible to achieve the things we want to achieve. Nor is it impossible to change from negative action to positive action and pursue our goals. But it requires belief. In Mark's gospel it says, "Whatever you ask for in prayer, believe that you have received it, and it will be yours" (11:24). I repeat what I said earlier: you only get one shot at life, so you may as well give it your best effort and make it as enjoyable, meaningful, adventurous, challenging, successful, and happy as you can.

The path to happiness was aptly worded by Albert Schweitzer:

I don't know what your destiny will be, but one thing I know: the only ones among you who will be really happy are those who have sought and found how to serve.

Indeed!

How to Value Your Everyday Life: Three Strategies

Today is the first day the rest of your life.

When I start my day, each and every day, I always remind myself to live my day to the very best of my abilities, so that when today becomes yesterday and tomorrow becomes today, I have no regrets. And how would you like to live your day? Here are three strategies on how to value your everyday life.

STRATEGY 1: Take One Day at a Time to Achieve Positive Things in Your Life

Live this day as though it were your last. Seneca said, "Begin at once to live, and count each day as a separate life." Indeed, what an encouraging piece of advice for wise living. Tomorrow may never come. Think about it. It might just save you for another new day.

Don't take tomorrow's problems for today's, because today has plenty of its own. Sometimes we see problems where there are no problems. Faith is hope in things unseen. Have faith and build your faith. It's good for the soul. "We walk by faith, not by sight," so the Bible says (2 Cor. 5:7).

Live today to the fullest, as if today is your *only* day. As German poet and philosopher Goethe said, "Nothing should be prized more highly than the value of each day."

Begin with the possible. Begin with one step, because there is always a limit. You cannot do more than you can. If you try to do too much, you will achieve nothing. Observe the law of moderation in all things. It is a safety measure.

You may have had the chance to read the book *Your Best Life Now* by the best-selling author Joel Osteen, the young, dynamic, humorous, happy, and always smiling pastor of Lakewood Church in Houston. Here is what he says:

> *Happy, successful, fulfilled individuals have learned how to live their best lives NOW. They make the most of the present moment and thereby enhance their future.*

You can, too, he says, no matter where you are or what challenges you are facing. You can enjoy your life right now! In fact, I want to share with you Joel Osteen's seven ways to live your life *now. Now*, he says, is the best way to live your life, not tomorrow, not yesterday—but *now*! And I'm happy to share with you some circumstances that show how Joel's ideas on how to live your best life now do really work—and could work for anyone who wants to live his or her best life—now! Cherish them in your heart and expect the best outcomes.

Joel Osteen's Seven Ways to Live Your Best Life Now

1. Enlarge your vision
2. Develop a healthy self-image
3. Discover the power of your thoughts and words
4. Let go of the past
5. Find strength through adversity
6. Live to give
7. Choose to be happy

I like it that Joel encourages you to enlarge your vision by "envisioning your success" and stop your wrong, negative thinking, which can keep you away from "God's best." He also says that you need to get into a positive mindset to perceive your vision before you receive, which is indeed very true.

To me, this is one way of using the Law of Attraction: *Whatever you perceive and believe, you can achieve.* When you discover the power of your thoughts and choose the right thoughts, you also reprogram your mental computer. And when you discover the power of your words and you speak life-changing words, you speak a blessing, too.

I totally agree with Joel when it comes to choosing your thoughts and words, because they have the power to make change possible and to produce better results in your life.

Some people do not know how to let go of past emotional hurts. But that is what you must learn: how to just "let go." Joel's advises you to let bitterness go, for when you do, you will somehow be rewarded and justified by God, who is also our ever-forgiving Father. This will enable change to take place in your favor, he says. To build your faith, you must expect to "see miracles."

I can relate to what Joel says here. Building my faith has brought both small and big miracles into my life. Faith will work in your life, too, if you build it. I believe that Joel is right when he says, "God has good things in store for you." I am a living witness of that. Always look at the bright side of life—smile—and things will fall into place before your very eyes! Build your faith!

He encourages you to find strength in your times of adversity. You need to get yourself up on the inside and always trust God's timing, for things happen for a reason. His message is this: our trials have purpose. In my many years of working as a professional social worker–counselor and private practitioner, I have seen many clients go through nasty times or find themselves in unfavorable circumstances in their lives and nevertheless hang on to their strength in those times of adversity. Naturally, I encouraged them to hold on to their strength, but I also tried to make them aware that this mental process requires both discipline and determination. It is not easy to pursue and achieve your purposes in the midst of difficult circumstances. But those who made the effort to work persistently on it emerged as winners in the end.

Dr. Robert Schuller illuminates this principle in his book *Tough Times Never Last, But Tough People Do*: God's delays are not God's denials. Hence, you have to trust God when you think that God does not make sense. Make sense?

What is called self-image, self-concept, or self-worth is very important to you, as well it should be, for anyone. "The me I see is the me I'll be," as the saying goes. Create a good image of yourself in your mind. And don't focus on your weaknesses. Focus instead on your God. See yourself as a winner, an overcomer, not the tail, but the head.

STRATEGY 2: Value Life

I recall a poignant story I read about Robert Allen, the author of *One Minute Millionaire* and other best-selling books. He described a bad car accident that he was in, an accident in which he could have easily died. And during his time of great pain, all he asked, he said was, "If only I could live for another day ..." That's how precious life is. When you lose it, it is gone forever. There is not another day to come. In his near-death experience, Robert Allen fittingly applied what Marcus Aurelius advocated:

> *When you arise in the morning, think of what a precious privilege it is to be alive—to breathe, to think, to enjoy, to love.*

Indeed, what a noble thought. Similarly, it is written in the best book of wisdom:

> *This is the day the Lord has made; let us rejoice and be glad in it. (Ps. 118:24)*

Value your life. Count your blessing anew each day. I remember my high school days. I attended an exclusive private school fifteen minutes away from our house. On the first Friday of the month, the school administrators gathered all the elementary and secondary students in the chapel for "First Friday" masses. I looked forward to these school activities, because when I was young I loved to sing. And I remember singing at the top of my voice the song "One Day at a Time, Dear Jesus." I also remember some of my classmates looking at me and smiling and giving me the thumbs up! It's wonderful how that song has stayed in my mind, reminding me every day to live life one day at a time.

The reading below was printed on a big white poster that I bought years ago from a bookstore in a large shopping center. It reminds you of some valuable ways to start your day.

This Day Is Yours—Use It Well!

This day is the day that belongs to me. It was given to me early in the morning freely and without obligation. The moment that I accepted the gift, I accepted the responsibility for its growth. I received it in good condition, fresh and clean, and now it is mine. I can choose what day it can become, I can make it ugly by deciding to be miserable, or I can make it beautiful by deciding to be glad.

This is the day to be happy. I know I just can be contented as I *wish to be.* Above all, I can find contentment now, instead of thinking it necessary to wait for some uncertain, future pleasure.

This is the day to be free to cut the bonds of all tomorrows and all those yesterdays. I would be unwise to waste any part of today on useless guilt or distress about a yesterday, or in pointless worry or panic about a tomorrow.

This is the day to treat life as an adventure and each moment of it as a satisfying, rewarding experience. Since I have but one chance of today, I want to live it fully, and I want to live it well. I hope that I will handle myself so that when today becomes yesterday, my memories will be pleasant, and when tomorrow becomes today, my regrets will be few. On this day, I do not want to indulge in crippling, selfish emotions such as anger, hatred, and fear; I want, instead, to seek their opposites.

This is the day to be thankful, for some pains removed and for some blessings received; to translate my gratitude from mere words into cheerful, wholehearted achievement.

This is the day I promise myself that I am going to build my world with gladness and with love—right now—because this is the ONLY DAY that belongs to me.

* * *

Johnny D. Wimbrey is a young and dynamic international motivational speaker and success coach and the founder and president of Wimbrey Training Systems. In his best-selling book *From the Hood to Doing Good,* he encourages you to find your "inner winner within." His message is simple yet powerful:

> *Your past doesn't determine your future—and if I can do it, anyone can.*

Indeed, what a powerful insight! I heard Johnny Wimbrey speak for the first time at a three-day international seminar in Australia that I attended, and I can tell you, Johnny is dynamite! When you hear him speak, you hang on to every word he says. I love what Johnny said about your "Personal Defining Moment" (PDM):

> *Your Personal Defining Moment is the moment you can say ... "I can—I'm in! I can do it!"*

This is the moment of truth that no one can take away from you. Have you found yet your "moment," your PDM? You are laser-focused that moment, he says, and time is something you can never get back. Your PDM may happen in two minutes or seventy-two hours. Winning begins within! Johnny concludes.

STRATEGY 3: Develop the Right Mental Attitude

They say that the right mental attitude makes all the difference between success and failure. In your journey toward achieving a successful and happy life, it is important to equip yourself with the right mental attitude.

I recently wrote an article entitled "Attitude Determines Your Happiness and Purpose in Life," published on EzineArticles.com. A positive and enthusiastic attitude, I wrote, could make a lot of difference between success and failure in one's life. Be positive in your attitude. Choose success.

Similarly, my thoughts and ideas on the scope of attitude have been reinforced by what I've read in the books of the evangelist and Bible teacher Jerry Savelle. His easy-to-read and easy-to-understand book *A Right Mental Attitude,* which offers "the doorway to a successful life," is in line with the views of other great writers and authors on the importance of having the right attitude. If every day you positively expect to overcome trials in your circumstances, you will emerge a winner. You will become an overcomer, and you will achieve peace and eliminate worries. Investing in your spiritual life and its benefits will enable you to live your daily life with inner peace, joy, and happiness. Your spirituality is an integral component of your overall happiness. Strengthen it!

Here are several tips to help you develop the right attitude.

Tip 1. Believe with your heart in the Gospel

"Put God's Word in your heart; put the Word in your heart." As you continue to inject God's Word into your heart, it will produce a very positive mental attitude in you. Tell yourself: "Yes, I love my God. He is my fountain of life and my Savior. He keeps me going day and night. Without Him, I am no one. But with Him, I can do everything. Christ is my strength."

Tip 2. Be a living epistle

Help someone get out of his or her mess or show them how.

Tip 3. Have faith in times of your trials

When problems come your way, your faith will help you overcome your worries. Let me repeat the verse that I alluded to earlier in this chapter: "Faith is being sure of what we hope for and certain of what we do not see" (Heb. 11:1).

> *Therefore, put on the full armor of God, so that when the day of evil [crisis] comes, you may be able to stand your*

ground, and after you have done everything [the crisis demands], to stand. Stand firm then, with the belt of truth around your waist. ... And take up the shield of faith, with which you can extinguish all the flaming arrows of the evil one. (Eph. 6:13–16)

Tip 4. "Take no thought" and live a worry-free life

Don't worry too much about the material necessities of life. In one of my weekly "Happiness Tips" newsletters, I mentioned to my subscribers that people understand the concept of happiness in many different ways. To some, happiness lies in the abundant accumulation of material things or in wealth or in comfort.

History tells us that two of America's richest men died lonely and unhappy: Howard Hughes and John Paul Getty. Billionaire Howard Hughes left a legacy of two billion dollars, yet spent most of his life as a recluse. At his death, he had no wife or children to mourn for him. Despite such wealth, his life produced tremendous loneliness.

John Paul Getty was another billionaire. It is believed he had accumulated from two to four billion dollars in the oil business. But his private life was unhappy. He was married and divorced five times, his youngest son died from pneumonia in 1953, and his eldest son died an alcoholic in 1973.

As we can see in the unhappy lives of these two famous American billionaires, abundance in everything may help, but it is *not* the be-all and end-all of a meaningful and happy life.

Tip 5. Resolve never to quit, never to give up, no matter what the situation

Later in this chapter, I share Pamela Owens Renfro's thoughts on not quitting. Let her words encourage you not to quit but keep on going!

Tip 6. Gird up the loins of your mind

A right mental attitude is of utmost importance in times of trouble.

Tip 7. Bring glory to God

Bertrand Russell, an atheist, paradoxically said, "Unless you assume a God, the question of life's purpose is meaningless."

Tip 8. Live God's avenue of faith; reject the devil's avenue of fear

Tip 9. Be righteous in all your ways

Tip 10. Offer the sacrifice of joy

When everything is against you, offer the sacrifice of joy.

Tip 11. Become strong-willed

Tip 12. Greatly rejoice

Goal-Setting and Your Dreams

You undoubtedly have your own personal goals and dreams. Whatever they are, surely you want to achieve your goals and fulfill your dreams. No matter what, there are two things to aim at in life:

Goal One: Get what you want.

Goal Two: Enjoy it.

They say only the wisest people achieve the second. Do you agree or disagree? Yesterday is the past and tomorrow is the future. Today is a gift, which is why they call it the *present*.

Be Strong and Don't Give Up

Pamela Owens Renfro

Remember ... There is a deeper strength and an
amazing abundance of peace available to you.
Draw from this well: call on your faith
to uphold you.

Realize that life is a series of levels, cycles of
ups and downs—some easy, some challenging.
Through it all, we learn; we grow strong in faith;
we mature in understanding.

The difficult times are often the best teachers,
and there is good to be found in all situations.
Reach for the good.

Be strong and don't give up!

Life is a movie you see through your own unique eyes. It makes little difference what's happening out there. It is how you take it that counts.

It is wise to think well, but planning well is wiser; however, doing well is wisest and the best of all.

Our life is what our thoughts make it. It is commonly said that waste of time is the most extravagant and costly of all expenses. That does make sense. So, use your time wisely. A life spent worthily should be measured by deeds, not by years, because the way you look at life dictates the way you live.

Marcus Aurelius once said that we have to confine ourselves to the present. And Eileen Caddy, in her book *The Dawn of Change,* instructs you to stop sitting there with your hands folded, looking on, doing nothing. You have to get into action and live this full and glorious life. Now! You just have to do it, she suggests.

There is a time for everything, and a season for every activity under heaven. (Eccl. 3:1)

You take this vision

every day of your life.

Look To This Day!

Look to this day!

For it is life.

The very life of life.

In its brief course

Lie all the verities and

Realities of your existence:

The bliss of growth

The glory of action

The splendour of beauty.

For yesterday is but

A dream and tomorrow is

only a vision.

Part of Buddhist philosophy teaches you that you shouldn't try to force anything; instead, you should just let go in life and see God opening millions of flowers every day without forcing the buds. However, this proverb sheds a different light on letting go in life:

Man cannot discover new oceans until he has the courage to lose sight of the shore.

Many take risks to pursue their goals; some make it, some don't. What matters is that you did give it a try! Someone has compared life to a wild tiger: you can either lie down and let it lay its paw on your head, or you can sit on its back and ride it.

Likewise, here is a reflection from Christopher Logue that can serve to remind you to move from inaction to action.

Come to the edge.
We might fall.
Come to the edge.

...

And he pushed
And they flew.

The above reflection indicates that nothing can be achieved without action and enthusiasm. To achieve success, fulfillment, and happiness, you must have the desire that triggers you to take action and to achieve positive outcomes from that action.

My philosophical and spiritual mind, coupled with my deep passion for life, attracts me to similar readings and thoughts on this subject.

In Susan Hayward's book of inspirational and spiritual quotes, *A Guide for the Advanced Soul*, she quotes sublime thoughts of Bhagwan Shree Rajneesh and Henry David Thoreau that are worth reflecting upon in the scheme of life:

We are not here just to survive and live long …

We are here to live and know life.

In its multi-dimensions;

To know life in its richness,

In all its variety.

And when a man lives

Multi-dimensionally,

Explores all possibilities available,

Never shrinks back from any challenge,

Goes, rushes to it, welcomes it,

Rises to the occasion,

Then life becomes a flame—

Life blooms.

—BHAGWAN SHREE RAJNEESH

THE SACRED "YES"

Go confidently in the direction of your dreams!

Live the life you've imagined.

As you simplify your life, the laws of universe

will be simpler;

Solitude will not be solitude,

Poverty will not be poverty.

Nor weakness weakness.

—HENRY DAVID THOREAU

This is the day to treat life as an adventure and each moment of it as a satisfactory, rewarding experience.

Live today as though it were

your last.

Power Word Number Two:

Love!

The greatest way to find love is to give love.

—Alan Loy McGinnis,

The Friendship Factor

What is Love?

The meaning of love is defined in numerous ways. There is no one definition of love. The definition can vary from person to person. Love can be subjective, depending on who is defining love and who is experiencing love. When we speak of love, keep in mind that *you must first love yourself before you can love another.*

By accepting yourself and joyfully being what you are, you fulfill your own abilities, and your simple presence can make others happy. That's what I call the nature of personal reality. Many great men and women of history and well-known authors have shared with us their own definitions of love. One of the world-renowned authors of our time, Dr. Denis Waitley, describes love this way:

> One definition of love, as a verb, is "to value." Love should be a verb, not a noun or adverb, because love is an active emotion. It is not static. Love is one of the few experiences in life that we can best keep by giving it away. Love is the act demonstrating value for and looking for the good in another person.

Stephen Covey shares Denis Waitley's notion that "love" is best seen as a verb. So does Rick Warren, who, in his book *The Purpose Driven Life* says that "Life is all about love and the best use of life is love."

Develop Your Ability to Love.

Even the greatest book of wisdom—the Bible—tells you that the greatest commandment is to love your neighbor as you love yourself. The apostle Paul writes that "faith, hope and love" are noble gifts, but "the greatest of these is love" (1 Cor. 13:13). Rick Warren acknowledges that life without love is really useless.

Love cannot be learned in isolation. *Relationships* are what life is all about, and love empowers you to reach higher levels in your relationships and in life. Doing what you love doing is the cornerstone of having abundance in your life. It is essential that you make a personal commitment to do what you love and love what you do—today, and every day of your life! This will also give continuity to what you are trying to achieve in your life.

Dr. James Lynch, scientific director of the Psychophysiological Clinic of Maryland School of Medicine, expresses his ideas on love in this thought:

> *Basically if you want to find love, you've got to give love.*

Similarly,

> *A loving person lives in a loving world. A hostile person lives in a hostile world. Everyone you meet is your mirror.*

The tenets of love seem difficult to practice in modern society. Maybe some will agree with me; maybe some will not. The question of what "true love" is can sometimes become subjective, depending who is experiencing it or who is talking about it.

As I mentioned earlier in this book, based on my years of experience as a professional social worker–counselor and a private practitioner in human organizations, I do believe that the modern world has deteriorated in its moral values. And my professional background in philosophy provides me with the ability to process deep knowledge and understanding, so that I am equipped with to deal with these daily human issues. You see exactly what is happening out there, but you need to go much deeper to understand the "why" of the issue and discover what must be done.

Analyzing our problems becomes a metaphysical process, and it may require structural strategies to solve them.

Why is love difficult to understand? I have observed that deep relationships are hard to establish and that easy, impersonal contacts are more common. The fact is, *love comes from within, not from without.* You have to want to love if you want to be loved back in return. You have to make a commitment to love if you want to receive back the rewards of love.

I definitely agree with the views and findings expressed by Dr. Lynch. I think if we are honest and aware of what's going on in our broad global society—or in many families and relationships, for that matter—we will agree that the values of modern society have deteriorated extensively from what they used to be. The value of good relationships, especially with respect to love, has diminished dramatically.

Four Factors to Consider in Love and Relationships

I have included four vital factors to consider in the domain of love and relationships: communication, trust, honesty, and giving.

The Communication Factor

Communication is pivotal. Open communication in a relationship is crucial to keep that relationship bloom, for it to take meaning and grow in positive dimensions towards a meaningful and happy relationship. As therapist in my field of expertise, I have dealt with all kinds of people: the rich, famous, and poor; very young children, youth, and the elderly; and professionals, laborers, and the unemployed. I have also helped people with non-English-speaking backgrounds who are marginalized and disadvantaged because they have difficulty communicating and yet want to understand other people and be understood themselves; people suffering from health issues; and people dissatisfied with their lives because of a lack of love in their relationships.

Gauging by the problems my clients experienced in their personal and family relationships, I came up with insights and strategies for how they or anyone experiencing similar issues in his or her life can improve and create more meaningful relationships with their families or people with whom they are connected.

First and foremost, make the extra effort to find quality time for improving family relationships. Contribute to creating a loving atmosphere, one that promotes individual growth, mutual appreciation for one another, generosity toward one another, and love for one another. It takes one family member to make a difference, someone who makes a conscious effort to make one positive contribution for the benefit of forming a more wholesome relationship and coming together in a more loving and peaceful atmosphere. The process of working things out together as family through thick and thin and pulling things together to make it work builds strength of spirit and of will.

Many of you may have been blessed to grow up in stable families that provide a solid foundation for your life. Count your blessings. However, also remember that the trials you face in life can provide the challenges that will build your character and strength, enabling you to rise from mediocrity and up the ladder of success. Experience, they say, is your greatest teacher.

I experienced firsthand a stable and happy family life. I grew up in a big family—six girls and three boys—with loving parents who served as our role models and with brothers and sisters who loved and helped one another in good times and in bad times. We managed to establish and maintain a stable and happy family life, respecting one another and protecting each other's best interest.

If you seek a more loving relationship where communication is vital, the above measures may help you find what you are looking for. On this matter, I therefore say:

> *To experience a truly happy, meaningful, and loving relationship in your life, a loving atmosphere in your home is a vital foundation for your life.*

> —Letty R. Vendramini

Good communication is one of the most critical areas in our efforts to build strong relationships.

Contrary to all our natural instincts, true fulfillment and happiness come from giving of ourselves, a belief that Rick Warren so strongly believes and teaches. So, take his suggestion and practice giving of yourself.

Risk is always a part of love. In the circumstances of your life, you may have experienced risks of myriad kinds. This is a powerful truth in the sphere of loving and relationships. C. S. Lewis acknowledged this truth in his book *The Four Loves* when he wrote:

> *To love all is to be vulnerable. Love anything and your heart will certainly be wrung and possibly be broken. If you want to make sure of keeping it intact, you must give your heart to no one, not even to an animal. Wrap it carefully around with hobbies and little luxuries, avoid all entanglements. Lock it up safe in the casket or coffin or your selfishness. But in that casket—safe, dark, motionless, airless—it will change. It will not be broken; it will become unbreakable, impenetrable, irredeemable.*

The alternative tragedy, or at least to the risk of tragedy, is damnation. The only place outside heaven where you can be perfectly safe from all the dangers and perturbations of love is hell.

Words to Forget, Words to Remember

The following are a few words and expressions you should either delete from or add to the vocabulary of your daily communication.

Words to Forget	*Words to Remember*
I can't	I can
I'll try	I will
I have to	I want
I should have	I will do
could have	my goal

someday	today
if only	next time
yes, but	I understand
problem	opportunity
difficult	challenging
stressed	motivated
worried	interested
impossible	possible
I, me, my	you, your
hate	love

The Trust Factor

In the sphere of love, trust is another vital element. In fact, as some would tell you, it is primarily trust that enables you to communicate in loving ways and makes you understand and empathize with the other side of the equation. Dr. Irwin M. Marcus, Clinical Professor of Psychiatry at Louisiana State University Medical School, puts it quite succinctly:

> *Out of trust comes honest communication and understanding, so for a relationship without this, two people cannot equally know each other; genuine trustworthiness is a wonderful quality to possess and find in a relationship, and is a cornerstone from which good communication can be built.*

We have seen how some well-known authors and models in the world defined love. It is important that you realize that in order to maintain a long and lasting relationship that is meaningful and loving, the vital ingredients of communication and trust must be kept altogether intact.

C. S. Lewis admonishes you to stop letting fear determine how you communicate in your relationships. No matter how much you want to be loved, you can only be loved to the extent to which you allow your "real self" to be known.

Love extends to forgiving your enemies. We read that we ought to forgive our enemies, but we do not read that we ought to forgive our friends as well. And he who has not forgiven has never yet tasted one of the most sublime enjoyments of life.

There is an old Native American proverb that goes like this: Before you criticize another brave person, you must walk a mile in his moccasins. How true, indeed! Getting into the mind and heart of another person is important. Contrary to many people's opinions, the major problem in a dating relationship is not poor communication. It is lack of understanding. You can have all the right techniques of communication, but it will be hollow if you are not committed to genuinely understanding or identifying with the other person.

After all, God became human to communicate with us and to teach us about right living and relationships with both himself and others.

The Honesty Factor

In a relationship, what your partner wants to discover is not only your head but also your heart. In every stage of a relationship, there is some level of vulnerability that gives you the freedom to express both thoughts and feelings. It is here that Jesus leads us by his example. He was transparent and honest, so much so that many people had a hard time accepting what he said.

All of us want to be known for who we really are. Who wants to love a false image, a mask someone is wearing? We are all afraid of rejection. In maintaining commitment, it is important to know that truth and love are inseparable in developing and maintaining commitment.

It is indeed amazing what love can do to people. In *The Friendship Factor*, Roy Alan McGinnis suggests you open up even the dark side of your life. Here is how he summed up his thoughts: "I can go so far as to say that you can never genuinely know yourself except as an outcome of discovering yourself to another person; you learn how to increase contact with your real self." That's powerful statement! That's self-awareness, too.

The Giving Factor

The word "give" is one of the seven power words in this book and will be more extensively discussed in chapter six. Here, however, I want to discuss it in the context of love and relationships.

I am a person who loves to give without counting the cost. In my family, we learned the value of this at a very young age, and we practiced it as we lived our lives in an atmosphere of love and giving, I and my five sisters (myself the youngest of the girls), three brothers, and our father and mother.

Giving is a positive habit that benefits both the giver and the receiver. However, others may construe giving as something done not only for the sake of giving but for what comes with the act of giving. In fact, many of those who are not used to this generous exercise of giving would claim that giving is costly. Many claim that giving improves one's image. McGinnis, for example, says:

> *One of the most effective ways to improve your self-image is*
> *to give of yourself to others in healthy, positive ways.*

However, there was one person who did not give in order to improve his image—Jesus. He gave without counting the cost. He gave his time to cure the sick, help the needy, and feed the hungry. He gave the water of life to the woman at the well. And, above all, he gave his own life so that we do not have to carry the heavy burden of our sins and our own failures. Now that's commitment.

How do you describe the people you value most in your life? Takers? Or givers? Most of us cherish the givers. They give their love to us freely; they give their time; they give us encouragement and support. Are you that kind of person in your relationships?

There may be times when you feel quite unloved. That is when you need to give the most. True sacrificial giving is not always based on how one feels; often it must be an act of one's will. One reason why you find it hard to make commitments may be that you are unwilling to pay the price.

> *The greatest way to find love is to give love.*

We can therefore say that in any lasting relationship, you need empathy, understanding, trust, and a basic love.

Giving to others is a key principle for building relationships. However, St. Augustine noted one more salient aspect of giving when his very close friend, Neridus, died and he felt crushed with grief. After loss of his friend, he said:

> *This is what comes ... of giving one's heart to anything but God. All human beings pass away. Do not let your happiness depend on something you might lose.*

Are you giving unselfishly in your relationships? Here are some questions you should ask yourself: Do you really have a giving spirit, giving to others as much as you do to the closest person in your life? Is it time for visits to the blind, elderly, and the sick? Do you give of your talents to the church? Do you share your personal relationship with Christ with others in need? Do you actively give love and kindness to your parents and family members?

The greatest way to find love is to give love.

For Christians, it is through a committed relationship with Jesus that we can best understand and develop a healthy relationship with another human being. Why? Because we focus on Jesus. He helps us get rid of selfishness, anger, weakness, and sin. Committing ourselves to Jesus changes everything, because he changes us, helping us to become more like him. This is Christ's promise:

> *I tell you the truth, whoever hears my word and believes him who sent me has eternal life and will not be condemned; he has crossed over from death to life. (John 5:24)*

Christ provides us with the *best* example in every area of commitment. But even more exciting, he's concerned about every other area and need in your life. He wants to guide you in close, happy, lasting relationships. He even promises to stand by you if your relationships break up.

Washington Irving is known for a famous quote that I often use when I speak of unreciprocated love:

> *Love is never lost. If not reciprocated, it will flow back and*
> *soften and purify the heart.*

This is true, indeed, for those of you who have experienced what he meant. In *Desiderata*, you are forewarned about love in these words:

> *Love is a gift that we all share—as friends, as family, as*
> *all creatures living together in this wonderful earth. And*
> *love, like a river, will cut a new path whenever it meets an*
> *obstacle. We are not the light, but by reflecting the light, we*
> *may bring hope and joy to others. Fighting weakens while*
> *harmony strengthens and empowers.*

William James said, "When you are good to others, you are best to yourself." When you have purpose in your life, it is also about loving and giving. Our lives are what our thoughts create.

Be yourself. Especially do not feign affection. Neither be cynical about love, for in the face of all aridity and disenchantment, it is as perennial as the grass.

—*DESIDERATA*

Love Is Patient

Love is patient
and kind, never jealous
or envious, never boastful
or proud, never haughty
or selfish or rude.
Love does not demand
its own way.
It is not irritable or touchy.
It does not hold grudges
and will hardly even notice
when others do it wrong.
It is never glad
about injustice,

but rejoices whenever
truth wins out.
If you love someone,
you will be loyal to him
no matter what the cost.
You will always believe
in him, always expect
the best of him,
and always stand your
ground in defending him.
All the special gifts and powers
from God will someday
come to an end but love goes on forever.

—1 Corinthians 4:5–8

LOVE: Letters to Live By

The *now* is the working unit of loving in your life. I believe that if you genuinely love or at least send kind thoughts to persons or things, these will change before your eyes.

Denis Waitley has lovingly created his "Love Letters to Live By." His principles enhance the whole loving process. Take note and practice them. His love letters have become part of my daily loving relationships. They work. Implement them to live a loving relationship every day of your life.

Love Letters to Live By

L   is for Listen. To love someone is to listen unconditionally to his values and needs without prejudice.

O   is for Overlook. To love someone is to overlook the flaws and the faults in favor of looking for the good.

V   is for Voice. To love someone is to voice your approval of him on a regular basis. There is no substitute for honest encouragement, positive "strokes" and praise.

E   is for Effort. To love someone is to make a constant effort to spend time, to make the sacrifice, to go to the extra mile to show your interest.

Self-esteem and Self-worth

Loving yourself is part of good self-esteem. Remember what I said in the introduction: "you cannot love others until you can love yourself first." Both Waitley and McGinnis agree with the idea that self-image is loving yourself first. I share their views, because I live it, too.

- Loving requires independence and is based on the ability to share ourselves with others out of choice, not out of independent need.

- True love is that relationship which is formed by two individuals who have the ability to sustain themselves separately.

- Only independent people are free to choose to stay in a relationship.

- People who are dependent remain in a relationship out of necessity.

A common observation regarding this twenty-first century is that society has changed in its core values, so much so that immediate gratification is predominant. Hence, many people are unable to express themselves in spontaneous and intimate relationships. Intimacy has disappeared, but sex is rampant. It is important to share values and care for each other. As the saying goes: *A touch is worth a thousand words. It makes a world of difference.* If you really want to be loved in life, you must first be loveable.

There is no such thing as love on demand, nor is love merely what you promised ten years ago to someone when you said you would always love him or her. *Love is a daily, mutual exchange of value.* Always remember that. Nothing transmits value so clearly as the physical touch. Use your sense of touch generously. Touch is the magic wand of intimacy. Love is keeping in touch. Develop the magic of touch. Reach out today, tonight, tomorrow, and every day for the rest of your life. If we want to be loved, we need to communicate in positive, loveable language. Take a moment to listen.

Expect the best;
Convert problems into opportunities;
Be dissatisfied with the status quo;
Focus on where you want to go,
Instead of where you are coming from;
And most importantly,

Decide to be happy,

Knowing it is an attitude,

A habit gained from daily practice and not a result or payoff.

—DENISE WAITLEY, *THE WINNER'S EDGE*

Above all else, guard your heart, for

it is the wellspring of life.

—PROVERBS 4:23

Power Word Number Three:

Think!

To find yourself, think for yourself.

—SOCRATES

The Law of Attraction

Whatever the mind can conceive and believe, it can achieve.

This powerful verse is what the Law of Attraction is all about. There is no doubt in the world about the phenomenal success of the movie *The Secret*, which popularized the Law of Attraction. Any knowledgeable person on the planet can use the principle to achieve positive things in every area of his or her life.

Many great men of the past used it, and thinkers of today are still using it. Napoleon Bonaparte applied in his era, and Clement Stone implemented it in his successful business ventures.

It is all about mindset. It is all about thoughts. It is creating your thoughts and believing that whatever you command your thoughts to do, you can achieve. Thoughts are things.

My studies of Western and Eastern philosophies have shaped the way I think today. I must say that I have been deeply influenced by the great wisdom of well-known philosophers, thinkers, religious leaders, and famous writers. They have provided me with an abundance of inspiration, a boundless source of uplifting and wise words and deep insights about life. Their wisdom has honed my thinking and creative abilities. They have articulated worthwhile ideals to live for, and they can serve as pillars of strength and guidance in your pathway to finding something worthwhile to live for.

You now live in the twenty-first century. You live in an age and time when phenomenal things happen in the world in just one flick of a finger. Viral technology has dramatically exploded and is apparently helping mankind in millions of different ways. The rapid advance of technology has in many ways made life both easier and also much more complicated. Those who know what they do with it are lucky; those who do not know how to cope with the advance of technology are left behind.

The advance of modern technology has not encouraged society to value deep thinking. Everything is at your fingertips and requires little thought. Hence, the thinking process is left untapped and may sink into oblivion.

Having said that leads me to the topic of this chapter: Think. In my view, this new age stifles the process of deep thinking. This is the opposite of our great men and women of history, who were deep thinkers.

We are what we think. All that we are arises from our thoughts. With our thoughts, we make the world. If you speak and act with a pure mind, happiness will follow you and your shadow becomes unshakeable.

Man is believed to be the only thinking species on the planet, though there have been reports of research claiming that the entertaining dolphins can "think," and perhaps a tiny percentage of other animals. But how do we think? How do humans think?

Think Rationally

Perhaps the most important thing in today's information age that is viewed as crucial for the educated person who must cope with a rapidly changing high-tech world is the skill of critical thinking. When people know how to think, it improves their quality of life and also their professional lives. Even the young generation is skilled nowadays in the digital world. We are all products of the thinking that's going on around us.

However, you must raise your standards of thinking, learning, and creativity, particularly if you want to be good at something. It is essential that both the younger and older generations develop their thinking abilities in order to achieve success in their lives. You have to equip yourself with knowledge, skills, and proper attitudes to achieve the results you want. You have to learn how to think.

Plant seeds today to equip yourself for tomorrow, and you never have to worry about the future again.

I remember four long years of deep and logical thinking during my university days, when I was working toward my bachelor's degree in philosophy and English. My classes in logic and metaphysics were very challenging and interesting to me. Students were taught rigorous, logical thinking and had to exercise these thinking methods in classroom argumentation and debate. I embraced the challenge of working out the highly difficult mental exercises that my professors gave us.

I methodically learned how to think deep thoughts and contemplate ideas in the metaphysical realm, a realm far beyond the physical sphere that you see with your naked eyes. And I was excited by discussing, arguing, and debating universal issues during our classroom sessions. In the process, I learned to become a philosophic person and to be open to other points of view espoused by other people. It taught me how to be open to things that are new.

I learned especially throughout those four university years how the mind works, how we understand things, how we can think of what we want to think about, and how we can achieve the things we want to achieve by using our mental powers in the right, positive ways. And I can say with great confidence that I honed the thinking skills that have enabled me to achieve the things I wanted to achieve in my life and become the success I have become in many areas of my life.

One of the outstanding ideas that stuck in my mind after finishing my degree is an idea that one of my philosophy professors lectured on in our class. Indeed, I still find it powerful. My professor said:

The human mind, once stretched by a new ambition, never returns to its original dimension.

That's a powerful idea to me! If this inspires you, you have reasons to think and move forward in order to achieve your ambitions in life, reach your goals, and fulfill your dreams! Make them come alive! Stretch your mind and live your dreams!

Perception and Communication

You may have read or come across some very interesting works that deal with the processes of human thinking and communication. Let me take the example of the number one national bestseller, *The Seven Habits of Highly Effective People* by Stephen R. Covey. Covey says that while he was involved in leadership development work and while he prepared bi-monthly programs on the subject of communication, he became particularly interested in "how communication and perception were formed and how they govern the way we see, and how the way we see governs the way we behave."

Covey's theory to me sounds akin to the Law of Attraction. Covey used "expectancy theory" and the idea of "self-fulfilling prophecies" (also known as the "Pygmalion effect") to demonstrate how deeply embedded our perceptions are. In addition, Covey adds that "we must look at the lens through which we see the world, as well as at the world we see, and that the lens itself shapes how we interpret the world." Powerful thought, indeed! This is a piece of wisdom worth implementing.

I like how Covey uses the metaphor of a lens. You definitely use your lens to see the world, but what you see depends on how you adjust the lens. Most of us adjust it specifically to see the "world" that we "expect" to see, not the bigger picture of the world. You therefore focus only on what you want to focus on, which may only be a small part of this vast world. By focusing the lens, you achieve what you perceive or expect to achieve; it is self-fulfilling because you are focused on expecting and fulfilling only what you expected to achieve.

My interpretation of Covey's theory basically reflects the Law of Attraction, explained in somewhat different terms. How you communicate your perception affects the results of what you want to achieve.

"Core-Level Mental Triggers"

For more than a year now, I have enjoyed reading Mike Brescia's regular newsletters, which are available online to subscribers at his website, ThinkRightNow.com. Brescia says that in his programs he has been helping people all over the world "to quickly make the kind of changes in their thoughts and actions that rocked their worlds." I'm sure he's right.

His newsletters, which circulate globally among his subscribers, have also had a tremendous impact on my thought patterns. Even in my day-to-day thinking and actions, they have given me strategies for positive actions and outcomes in what I want to achieve. His presentation of "core-level mental triggers" is helpful to anyone seeking ways of thinking that can make changes for the better. I am grateful to Mike Brescia for his wonderful contribution to good thinking.

I am sure his ideas are helping a lot of people in making their lives better, as they helped him become a big success. To prove his point, he had the audacity to tell to the whole world that he was a failure who hit rock bottom. He admitted that he was homeless and lived in a nine-year-old 1978 Ford E-150 van. Living a life of failure made him desperate. But he "went from a lifetime of failure, anxiety, depression and alcoholism to a confident, sober internationally known business success in less than two years."

He says the success he desired depended on self-belief, determination, willpower, and persistence, but he said he did not find them. He added:

> *Socially, physically, mentally, career ... You name it, everything in my life changed, because I changed my minute-by-minute thoughts, my core beliefs about myself.*

According to alexa.com, Think Right Now is currently "the most visited personal development site on earth." His audio programs "force" the success and happiness. You might also want to learn more from his site and how he thinks his way to success and happiness.

I also recommend his site if you want to let go of anger, jealousy, resentment, fear, doubt, anxiety, or depression. It shows you how to find your will and your drive to do what you know you should do. Simply said, it empowers your thoughts and actions so that you can achieve positive outcomes in whatever it is you want to do, and it will help ensure that your choices are the right choices a lot more often. Thus, it will take you toward greater and greater accomplishments.

Brescia talks about changes that happen in people when they alter the "core-level mental triggers" that create the specific emotions that control what your attitudes and actions will be. His success conditioning programs retrain your brain and regroove the basic mental patterns that control what you do and how well you do it. I commend Brescia for his powerful ideas that help individuals think for themselves—and for the better.

It is vitally important that we develop positive attitudes for better thinking.

The Magic of Music

Studies done at the Center for the Neurobiology Learning and Memory at the University of California, Irvine shows that "slow, rhythmic 'mathematical' 60 BPM music puts you into the perfect state of mind and body for learning new mental patterns like nothing else … internalized into the fabric of who you are."

As popular as the Law of Attraction defined in the book *The Secret* is, let's keep in mind that "all successes come from behaviors … from doing something … simple as that."

It is a fact that all behaviors start out as thoughts (mental activity). So if you want different behaviors, you'll need to have different thoughts.

Beyond the achievement of minimal competence, sometimes it is essential to develop what are often called "higher order" thinking skills, refined by analytical and critical thinking and perception.

Problem-solving skills, sound reasoning in understanding, and making complex choices are all part of the thinking process. Decisions and choices are complex basic thinking skills that start at a very young tender age.

Critical thinking is referred to as "the gold standard" of critical thinking tests and powerful problem-solving techniques.

Critical Thinking

In 1605, Francis Bacon aptly described critical thinking in this manner:

> *For myself, I found that I was fit for nothing so well as for the study of Truth; as having a mind nimble and versatile enough to catch the resemblances of things; as being gifted by nature with desire to seek, patience to doubt, fondness to meditate, slowness to assert, readiness to consider, carefulness to dispose and set in order; and as being a man that neither affects what is new or admires what is old, and that hates every kind of imposture.*

A shorter version is: The Art of Being Right.

Or, more prosaically,

> *Critical thinking is the skillful application of a repertoire of validated general techniques for deciding the level of confidence you should have in proportion to the light of the available evidence.*

Many thinkers have studied the area of critical thinking. Here are some of their definitions of critical thinking:

Robert Innis: "Critical thinking is reasonable, reflective thinking that is focused on deciding what to believe or what to do."

Alec Fisher and Diodenus Scriven: "It is the skilled and active interpretation and evaluation of observations and communications, information and argumentation."

Edward Glaser: "An attitude of being disposed to consider in a thoughtful way the problems and subjects that come within the range of one's experiences." Edward Glaser points out below the necessary skills to apply his definition of critical thinking:

(1) It includes the ability to generate questions, construct and recognize the structure of arguments, and adequately support arguments.

(2) Define, analyze, and devise solutions for problems and issues;

(3) Sort, organize, classify, correlate materials and data;

(4) Integrate information and see relationships;

(5) Evaluate information, materials, and data by drawing inferences, arriving at reasonable interpretations, suspending beliefs, and remaining open to new information, methods, cultural systems, values and beliefs, and by assimilating information.

According to Brooke Noel Moore and Richard Parker, critical thinking is "the careful, deliberate determination of whether we should accept, reject, or suspend judgment about a claim, and the degree of confidence with which we accept or reject it."

Critical thinking is judging information that we are confronted with. You can also try to ask better questions yourself. You can always become a better thinker. Learn how to think more effectively and generate creative solutions in all aspects of your life.

I read something that went this way: "You can lead students to get thinking skills, but you can't make them think. They have to think for themselves."

American actress and politician Helen Douglas (1900–80), who became a Broadway star at the age of twenty-two, pointed out and strongly stressed what all of us already know: character is not inherited. One builds it daily by the way one thinks and acts, thought by thought, action by action, she said. If one lets fear or hate or anger take possession of the mind, they become "self-forged chains."

Robert Valett's "The ABCs of Happiness," from his *Prescriptions of Happiness*, encourages you to:

1. Imagine great things
2. Question most things
3. Think rationally
4. X-ray and carefully examine problems

What you may be thinking and planning for your life may *not* be what the Creator of the Universe has planned for you. Maybe you should get down on your knees and ask, "What would Jesus do?"

Let me add the Biblical proverb that says,

> *Many are the plans in man's heart, but it is the Lord's purpose that prevails. (Proverbs 19:21)*

On another note, Ralph Waldo Emerson said:

> *Conversation enriches the understanding, but solitude is the school of genius.*

Whatever the mind can conceive and believe, it can achieve.

Anyone who stops learning grows old, whether at twenty or eighty but, anyone who keeps learning stays young. The greatest thing in life is to keep your mind young.

If you can transform your thinking,

you can transform your life.

—Romans 4:12

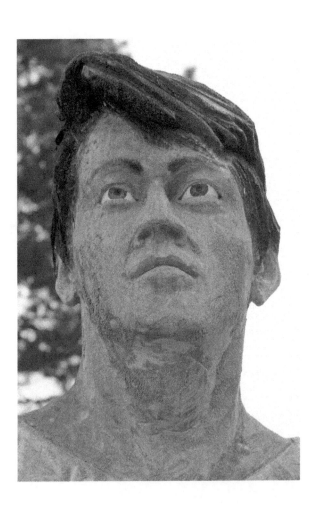

To find yourself, think for yourself.

-SOCRATES, GREEK PHILOSOPHER

chapter 4

Power Word Number Four:

Learn!

The only really happy people are those who have learnt how to serve.

—RICK WARREN,

THE PURPOSE-DRIVEN LIFE

Taking the Opportunity to Learn

Carlyle said that "every noble work seems at first impossible," and I believe that many of you would readily agree. He further stressed his point when he said that this is the reason why "the golden moments in the stream of life rush past us and we see nothing but sand; the angels come and visit us, and we only know when they are gone."

Carlyle must have known human nature all too well to have said what he said. If you look back in your life, how many occasions do you think you missed that might have been your "golden moments" had you not thought them insignificant and taken action on them? Someone has said that the little things in life that we seem to see as little are, in the end, the big things. By not taking action, you fail to learn to take advantage of the opportunities that come into your life.

However, you ought to remember that the conditions of conquest are always easy:

> *We have but to toil awhile,*
> *Endure awhile,*
> *Believe always, and*
> *Never turn back.*

That's the challenge you have to accept.

If you want success in this world, you must make your own opportunities as you go along in life. Persistent people always end with success, while others end in failure. Why? Because people who fail don't want to take the risk of doing something out of their comfort zones. They fear failure. They fear trying something new. They fear discomfort. They fear change. But when you take a risk and do something outside of your comfort zone and fail, that's when failure becomes your greatest teacher. When you try and fall, rise again until you succeed. That's learning for you.

Every mistake is a learning opportunity only if you learn from it.

Embrace your problems instead of resisting them. Ask yourself what potential lessons you learn from them.

Learn with Purpose

"Purpose is the engine that powers our lives," wrote Denis Waitley in his book *Seeds of Greatness: The Ten Best-kept Secrets of Total Success.*

He explains that the mind is goal seeking *by design.* He says that successful individuals have game plans and purposes that are clearly defined and to which they constantly refer. They know where they are going every day, every month, and every year. Things don't just happen in their lives. They make things happen for themselves and for their loved ones. They know goal-achieving actions and activities that are tension relieving.

This may mean personal growth, contribution, creative expression, loving relationships, and spiritual harmony that are the common goals that make us try to be uncommon people. So he suggests that "specific written goals are the tools which make purpose achievable." This is so because the mind is a bio-computer that needs definitive instructions and directions. Dennis Waitley adds: "We are told that the reason most people do not reach their goals is that they don't define them, earn them, or ever seriously consider them as believable or achievable."

Doing something that has meaning and purpose is more desirable than doing something that appears to be useless or a waste of time. "A quality life," he says, "is achieved through a balance in meeting the physical, social, mental and spiritual needs in an integrated way." Fulfillment in each area affects functioning in every other area of life. When people feel healthy, they can function better than if they are sick, hungry, or tired. Having a sense of belonging gives more motivation than feeling alienated, isolated, or alone. Being involved, stimulated, and challenged gives greater focus than doing simpler tedious tasks.

When you have the potential to learn certain skills, the learning can be enhanced by meeting all your basic needs. This happens even with children. Children, for that matter, learn potential skills and use communication devices to achieve something. Denis Waitley explains

> *If you don't tell your teacher what level you are by asking a question or revealing ignorance, you will not learn to grow and cannot pretend for long because you will finally be found out. Hence, admission of ignorance is the first step of our education.*

Learning to listen is one way to have effective relationships with your spouse, children, friends, and working associates. Listening involves patience, openness, and a desire to understand, which are highly developed qualities of character.

Stephen Covey discussed a "new level of thinking" of which Albert Einstein was proponent:

> *The significant problems we face cannot be solved in the same level of thinking we were at when we created them.*

If we look at Covey's book, it is all about a principle-centered, character-based "inside-out" approach to personal and interpersonal effectiveness. In Covey's words, "This means we start first with the self, but more fundamentally, we start with the most 'inside' part of the self—with our paradigms, our character, and our motives. Everything starts with the inner self. We have to be that kind of positive person to generate the energy if we want to accomplish anything. Keeping promises to others precedes keeping promises to ourselves, which sidesteps negative energy rather than empowering it."

Learning life skills can enhance a person's life, but they are not the be-all and end-all of happiness. Spending a lot of money or exercising life skills will not make a person happy unless he or she has a sense of belonging, friendships and relationships with others, good health, and is doing things that are desirable, meaningful, and purposeful. Through adaptations, supports, and interdependency, your quality of life need not be sacrificed if you cannot master life skills.

It is more important to help a child learn to use his or her abilities, than attempt to eradicate the disability.

Colleen F. Tomko shares her thoughts on children and the relationship of their skills, quality of life, and success on the website www.kidstogether. org. She says that "success needs to be measured in quality of life, not quantity of skills. Before any child's life can be enhanced with life skills, they need to first have a life."

I can fully relate to what she believes. In working as a social worker–counselor, as a therapist in human and community organizations, and as a private practitioner, I dealt with a lot of disadvantaged and marginalized children who came from various ethnic and religious backgrounds.

However, you have to carry on no matter what happens. Hold your private sorrows under a smile and carry on. *Be positive in what you want to learn and achieve in your life.* In the Bible, we read: "I can do everything through him who gives me strength" (Phil. 4:13). Get your faith and enthusiasm going!

But while it is wise to learn from experience, it is wiser to learn from the experiences of others. Anyone willing to be corrected is on the pathway to life. Anyone refusing has lost his chance.

Form good, positive habits. Habit is a cable. We weave a thread of it everyday, and at last we cannot break it. "A successful man is not he who has accomplished valuable things, but he who enjoys the work while accomplishing it." Dan Robey talks of positive habits in his book *The Power of Positive Habits.*

Remember that the key to everything is patience. You get the chicken by hatching the egg, not by smashing it. Until you dare to believe that there is something inside you that is superior to circumstance, nothing splendid will ever be achieved.

Walt Whitman, in *Leaves of Grass,* asks,

> *Have you learn'd lessons only of those who admired you, and were tender with you, and stood aside for you? Have you not learn'd great lessons from those who reject you, and brace themselves against you? or dispute the passage with you?*

We need criticism to keep us awake. It makes us see our weaknesses so that we may correct them. Well, it is also something you can avoid by saying nothing, doing nothing, and being nothing.

I remember someone asking me if prayer changes things. I replied, "No! Prayer changes people, and people change things."

Here is an encouraging thought and wisdom from the famous Pythagoras, who once said: "Rest satisfied with doing well, and leave others to talk of you as they will."

Everyone around you is your teacher. Learn your lessons quickly and move on.

I'd like to share with you the wisdom of Og Mandino on how to learn from faith and prayer. His prayer has had a big influence on my prayer habits since I read it first in 1988. My sister from the United States brought it for me when she came for holiday in Australia for Expo '88. I hope you too will learn something from his prayer, "The Scroll Marked X."

Learning From Faith and Prayer

Og Mandino poses these questions to you:

Who is of so little faith that in moment of great disaster or heartbreak has not called on his God? Who has not cried out when confronted with danger, death or mystery beyond his own experience or comprehension? From where has this deep instinct come which escapes from the mouth of all living creatures in moments of peril?

Move your hand in haste before another's eyes and his eyelids will blink. Tap another on his knee and his leg will jump. Confront another with dark horror and his mouth will say, "My God" from the same deep impulse.

Og Mandino tells you that all creatures that walk the earth, including man, possess the instinct to cry for help. And why do we possess this instinct, this gift, he asks?

He says that our cries are a form of prayer and these cries are heard by some superior power having the ability to hear and to answer our cry. Hence, he will pray, but ...

My cries for help will only be cries for guidance ... [not] for the material things of the world, ... not to a servant to bring me food, ... not ordering an innkeeper to provide me with room, ... [not to] seek delivery of gold, love, good health, petty victories, fame, success, or happiness. Only for guidance will I pray, that I may be shown the way to acquire these things, and my prayer will always be answered.

This is how he prays. This prayer was interpreted by Father Bob Garon in the way he thought fit. Father Garon's prayer can be found in the appendix.

I will pray for guidance, and I will pray as a salesman, in this manner—

Oh, creator of all things, help me. For this day I go out into the world naked and alone, and without your hand to guide me I will wander far from the path which leads to success and happiness.

I ask not for gold or garments or even opportunities equal to my ability; instead, guide me so that I may acquire ability equal to my opportunities.

You taught the lion and the eagle how to hunt and prosper with teeth and claw. Teach me how to hunt with words and prosper with love so that I may be a lion among men and an eagle in the market place.

Help me to remain humble through obstacles and failures; yet, hide not from mine eyes the prize that will come with victory.

Assign me to tasks which others have failed; yet, guide me to pluck the seeds of success from their failures.

Confront me with fears that will temper my spirit; yet, endow me with courage to laugh at my misgiving.

Spare me sufficient days to reach my goals; yet, help guide me in my words that they may bear fruit; silence me from gossip that none be maligned.

Discipline me in the habit of trying and trying again; yet, show me the way to make use of the law of averages; endow me with patience which will concentrate my strength.

Bathe me in good habits that the bad ones may drown; yet, grant me compassion for weaknesses in others. Suffer me to know that all things shall pass; yet, help me to count my blessings of today.

Expose me to hate so it not be a stranger; yet, fill my cup with love to turn strangers into friends.

But all these things be only if thy will. I am a small and lonely grape clutching the vine; yet, thou hast made me different from others. Verily, there must be a special place for me. Guide me. Help me. Show me the way.

Let me become all that you planned for me when my seed was planted and selected by you to sprout in the vineyard of the world.

Help this humble salesman

Guide me, God

Pythagoras also gave a beautiful insight saying that it was necessary to examine one's actions each day. He said:

Learn to be silent. Let your quiet mind listen and absorb.

> Anyone who stops learning grows old, whether at twenty or eighty, but anyone who keeps learning stays young. The greatest thing in life is to keep your mind young.

Wisdom Is Supreme

Proverbs 4

1   *Listen, my sons, to a father's instruction;*
    pay attention and gain understanding.

2   *I give you sound learning,*
    so do not forsake my teaching.

3   *When I was a boy in my father's house,*
    still tender and an only child of my mother,

4   *he taught me and said,*
    "Lay hold of my words with all your heart;
    keep my commands and you will live.

5   *Get wisdom, get understanding;*
    do not forget my words or swerve them.

6   *Do not forsake wisdom, and she will protect you;*

love her and she will watch over you.

7 *Wisdom is supreme; therefore get wisdom.*
Though it cost all you have, get understanding.

8 *Esteem her and it will exalt you;*
embrace her, and she will honor you;

9 *She will set a garland of grace on your head*
and present you with a crown of splendor."

10 *Listen, my son, accept what I say,*
and years of your life will be many

11 *I guide you in the new way of wisdom*
and lead you along straight paths.

12 *When you walk, your steps will not be hampered;*
when you ran, you will not stumble.

13 *Hold on to instruction, do not let it go;*
guard it well, for it is your life.

14 *Do not set foot on the path of the wicked*
or walk on the way of evil men

15 *Avoid it, do not travel on it;*
turn from it and go on your way.

16 *For they can not sleep till they do evil;*
they are robbed of slumber
till they make someone fall.

17 *They eat the bread of wickedness*
and drink the wine of violence.

18 *The path of the righteous if like the gleam of dawn,*
shining ever brighter till the full light of day.

19 *But the way of the wicked is like deep darkness;*

   they do not know what makes them stumble.

20 *My son, pay attention to what I say;*

   listen closely to my words.

21 *Do not let them out of your sight,*

   keep them within your heart;

22 *for they are life to those who find them*

   and health to a man's whole body.

23 *Above all else, guard your heart,*

   for it is the wellspring of life;

24 *Put away perversity from your mouth;*

   keep corrupt talk from your lips.

25 *Let your eyes look straight ahead,*

   fix your gaze directly before you.

26 *Make level paths for your feet*

   and take only ways that are firm.

27 *Do not swerve to the right or the left;*

   keep your foot from evil.

For the Lord gives wisdom, and from His mouth come knowledge and understanding.

—Proverbs 1:6

Power Word Number Five:

Give!

Perfect kindness acts without thinking of kindness.

— Lao Tzu

Giving Is an Art

What does it mean to give? And how must one give? One of the greatest challenges we face in our quest to enjoy our best lives now is the temptation to live selfishly.

This is what Gerald G. Jampolsky says about giving in his book *Love is Letting Go of Fear*: "Giving means extending one's Love with no conditions, no expectations and no boundaries." Peace of mind occurs, therefore, when we put all our attention into giving and have no desire to get anything from, or to change another person. The giving motivation leads to a sense of inner peace and joy that is unrelated to time.

Giving gives joy. You have to understand the importance of giving and the joy of giving. You do not need to be heroic and go to some distant land to find it.

The Hindu concept of *dana,* voluntary giving, has been the cornerstone of the spirit of volunteerism in India. Every act of giving is an act of non-greed, non-hatred, and non-delusion (*lobka, dosa, moha*). When you give, you have loving kindness. Do good and feel good. A tenet of the Buddhist scriptures in the Suttanta Pitaka is that the right way of giving alms as a meritorious action arises only from volition. *Without the will to give, there is no act of giving.*

People of all different backgrounds, life stages, and social strata have testified to the joy of giving. And to those who practice it and make it a way of life, it is indeed rewarding.

Khalil Gibran, in his book *The Prophet,* expresses a powerful thought on giving. He says:

> *There are those who give with joy, and joy is their own reward. And there are those who give with pain, and pain becomes their own baptism.*

The Universal Law of Giving and Receiving

When we give, we have to give lovingly, cheerfully, and joyfully. This we need to do to change our prosperity and abundance.

Searchgive.com presents a study on the biology of giving. It claims that it has been proven that we are hardwired for giving: pleasure areas in our brains activate when we give. A new study proves that when we choose the charity, the pleasure is even greater.

Deepak Chopra's *The Seven Spiritual Laws of Success*, defines the "laws of giving" as follows:

> *The universe operates through dynamic exchange ... giving and receiving different aspects of the flow of energy in the universe. And in our willingness to give that which we seek, we keep the abundance of the universe circulating in our lives.*

This is what Chopra writes about giving and the flow of money:

> *Because your body and your mind and the universe are in constant and dynamic exchange, stopping the circulation of energy is like stopping the flow of blood. Whenever the blood stops flowing, it begins to clot, to coagulate, to stagnate. That is why you must give and receive in order to keep wealth and affluence—or anything you want in life—circulating in your life.*

Let me also mention Deepak Chopra's idea of how money fits into the flow of things in our lives. He writes:

> *The word affluence means to "flow in abundance." Money is really a symbol of the life energy exchange and the life*

energy we use as a result of the service we provide to the universe. Another word for money is "currency," which reflects the flowing nature of energy. The word currency has its roots from the Latin word "curere" meaning, "to run" or "to flow." Therefore, if we stop the circulation of money—if our only intention is to hold on and hoard it— since it is life energy, we will stop its circulation back into our lives as well. Like a river, money must keep flowing; otherwise, it begins to stagnate, to clog, to suffocate and strangle its very own force. Circulation keeps it alive and vital.

Giving engenders receiving, and receiving engenders giving. In reality, receiving is the same as giving, because giving and receiving are different effects of the flow of energy in the universe.

Four Guides to the Law of Giving

To implement this law of giving (and therefore, receiving) in your life, Deepak Chopra suggests the following guides. I recommend that you test them in your own life.

Guide 1: Today, I will give something to everyone I come in contact with. I will give them each a gift. The gift may be a compliment, a flower, a prayer, a smile. At the end of the day, I will reflect on how I feel about the gifts that I gave.

Guide 2:   Today, I will gratefully receive all gifts that the universe has to offer me. I will say "Thank You, God" for the gifts of sunlight, of mountain breezes, of a child's smile. At the end of the day, I will reflect on how I feel about the gifts I received.

Guide 3:   Test out the Law and give cheerfully, joyfully, and lovingly. Experience the Law through the abundance of love, wealth and happiness that is yours to reap.

Guide 4:   The power of giving comes from a selfless act where you simply give from your heart. Jesus said in the Bible that "it is more blessed to give than to receive." It should not be seen as an onerous duty but a joyous privilege.

Using Your SHAPE in Giving

On another note, Rick Warren presents a different angle on giving of your self. He believes that

The greatest gift you can give someone is your time.

In his book *The Purpose-Driven Life*, he says that giving is in alignment with your purpose. Warren reminds us that when God gives us an assignment, he always equips us with whatever we need to accomplish it. This combination of capabilities he calls SHAPE: Spiritual Gifts, Heart, Abilities, Personality, and Experience. Nobody else can be me. God deserves your best. You will never know what you are good at until you try, he says, so use your SHAPE.

This is what he says about giving:

> *Give for the sake of giving and keep it circulating as it flows. When you give without expectation, it is genuine giving. When you give expecting something in return, you do not love wholeheartedly, you love conditionally.*

When you allow God to speak through you and smile upon the earth through you—because you are an unconditional giver, a purposeful being—prosperity will be your reward.

> *When you give—give and go on giving and never count the cost.*

Some give with the thought of getting something back—all the time. And when they don't get back what they expect in return, they turn sour, negative, and unhappy. That's not what a true giver is all about.

I just want to mention here that I learned at a very young age the generous ways of my long-deceased father. My father loved helping people. He'd even give away his very last cent just to help someone, even if it meant walking home or even going hungry. I saw him live his life giving generously to needy people without expecting anything in return. He loved to help the deprived and less fortunate citizens. It didn't matter to him if he gave his very last cent to help someone get from point A to point B.

He always taught us: "Money is not all. I like to share my blessings if it helps others meet their urgent needs and be happy." My father was known to people for his golden heart, and it is a great pleasure for me to make known to the world that I am very proud that I am also like my father, a person with a golden heart who loves to give and share with my family, my brothers and sisters, nieces and nephews, and humanity.

Writing this book is my way of personally acknowledging my dear father and his vital role in my life. My father passed away a very happy man in 1974 at age 65. He suffered an internal hemorrhage after he fell and hit his head on the concrete basement of our bathroom early one morning as he was preparing himself to attend the first day of the nine days before Christmas.

> *My long-deceased father, I salute you, and may your soul rest in peace. I love you, my dear father, and I thank you for all the core values you taught us in the family. You had a heart of gold when it came to giving without counting the cost and loving unconditionally. Thank you for being the role model for my life and for what I have become today.*

Like my father, I know the joys of giving and serving. I live them, too!

I love reading Khalil Gibran's famous book, *The Prophet*. When it comes to giving, this is what I learned from him, in his words:

> *You give little when you give of your possessions. It is when you give yourself that you truly give.*

I can relate to that. Can you? When you give of yourself—your time in helping people who need your help—that's the *best* help you can offer.

That's genuine help. Do you also give more of your possessions to help others or give of yourself more? Which path would you take? And in what manner will you do it?

"What the right hand giveth, the left hand receiveth back a thousandfold." I oftentimes hear my elder sister say this. She too is a giver, and I bless her for her good heart. I learned a lot from her. Her blessings are abundant and overflowing. We, too, can learn from this.

The joy of giving is indeed a gift, both for the giver and the receiver. Once again, I quote Joel Osteen, who talks about the joy of giving. He says that one of the seven ways to live "your best life now" is "live to give." In so doing, Osteen says, you have to live the joy of giving.

Show God's kindness and mercy and keep your heart of compassion open. You must learn how to be a giver and not a taker, because we were created to give. Whatever you give will be given back to you. "If you really want to thrive," says Osteen, "you must learn to be a giver." I can relate to what Osteen is saying here, because I know the joys of giving—to both the giver and the receiver of the gift. I have lived it all my life, and I also know the happiness it creates in my life and the lives of others.

You reap what you sow. As written in the Bible, "Whoever sows sparingly will also reap sparingly" (2 Cor. 9:6). And the reason why many people do not grow in abundance is because they do not sow. Do something out of the ordinary!

The joy of Living is the Joy of Giving.

—RICK WARREN,

The Purpose-Driven Life

There are those who give with joy
and joy is their reward.

- KAHLIL GIBRAN

chapter 6

Power Word Number Six:

Laugh!

They say I will laugh at the world.

—Og Mandino,
The Greatest Salesman in the World

Scope and Limitations

I n this chapter on laughter, my primary intention, as the author of the book, is merely to present and inform you, the reader, about two major topics: what laughter is and the gender differences in laughter. I did not therefore initially intend to adopt a funny or humorous tone, yet I did want to inform you about laughter and tell you that what makes men laugh may not necessarily have the same effect on women.

But for readers who expect more than just information and would also like a bit of fun and laughter, I have included five jokes that I think will make you laugh and thus bring fun and laughter into your life at least while you are reading this chapter. The jokes I have included exemplify some of the given meanings of "laughter." So be ready to laugh, laugh some more, and keep on laughing until you finish reading the jokes. You can also share these jokes with your friends, with your workmates during break time, at family gatherings, at social get-togethers, and on almost any occasion.

After reading the jokes, I will ask you to write down ten things that make you laugh. In the end, you will realize the feeling of happiness and well-being that comes when you laugh and laugh some more, every day of your life.

Eileen Caddy, and other authors as well, said that "you grow up the day you have the first real laugh—at yourself!"

Let there be more joy and laughter in your living.

To make laughing a truly effective workout, it is thought that one must laugh at least thirty seconds. We must always keep a sense of humor and be able to laugh at ourselves. I just believe, myself, that if you want to be successful in your life, you must be able to laugh at yourself. It will help you cope with the difficulties of life. We learn how to live and love, to think, to learn, and to give, but we also must learn how to laugh.

As the saying goes, "laughter is the best medicine." This is commonly believed. I believe that this is true in many ways. Laughter, for example, eliminates the toxins in your system, making you healthier, and thus allows you to live much longer and enjoy life better.

But what is laughter? Or humor? Laughter or humor can be looked at in many different ways in the science of gelotology, which is the study of humor and laughter and their psychological and physiological effects. Below are definitions of laughter and descriptions of it in various contexts.

What is Laughter?

Laughter is an expression or appearance of merriment or amusement. One very good example of this is the clown, which appeals so much to young children and amuses them.

Laughter is a sound that can be heard. It may ensue (as a physiological reaction) from jokes, tickling, and other stimuli. We of course get into these situations in a variety of ways. We have comedians and humorists. Even simple sounds from animals can trigger laughter in both the young and not so young.

Laughter can be induced by nitrous oxide; other drugs, such as cannabis, can also induce episodes of strong laughter. The explosion of a balloon is one good example. Don't all kids want to play this game! But no, even adults play this game on happy occasions, be it birthdays, game time, weddings, and many more that you can think of.

Strong laughter can sometimes bring about tears or even moderate muscular pain as a physical response to the act, due to muscular atrophy. Reaching the top of Mt. Everest is a glorious event to any mountaineer, as is winning the final lap of a marathon; these and similar event can trigger laughter and bring you to the verge of tears. It is the joy and happiness of the moment. It is the sense of victory and fulfillment, jubilantly proclaimed to the world: "I made it!"

Laughter can also be a response to physical touch, such as tickling, or even to a moderate pain, such as pressure on the ulnar nerve or the funny bone, as they call it.

Laughter is a part of human behavior regulated by the brain. It helps humans clarify their intentions in social interaction and provides an emotional context to conversations. Some become participants in this type of laughter, while others become observers of this process.

Laughter is a sign of being part of a group; it signals acceptance and positive interaction. "No man is an island," so the saying goes. And for that matter, you always belong to a group, be it your circle of close friends, your family, your church members, your coworkers, or your professional team or allies. When you belong to a group, you can feel free to laugh to your heart's delight when you feel like it, and the people in your group will most likely laugh with you and share your laughter, and they often react positively.

Laughter often seems contagious; the laughter of one person can itself provoke laughter in others. This may account in part for the popularity of laugh tracks in situation comedy television shows. When I find some time to relax at home, I prefer to watch a comedy television show. It also loosens frazzled nerves and makes you relax even more.

Laughter, sometimes known as chuckling, might not be confined or unique to humans, despite Aristotle's observation that "only the human animal laughs." The difference between chimpanzee and human laughter may be the result of the adaptations that evolved to enable human speech.

I learned in my psychology classes that some behavioral psychologists argue that self-awareness of one's situation or the ability to identify with another's predicament are prerequisites for laughter, and thus certain animals are not laughing in the human manner.

I did some research in Wikipedia, the free online encyclopedia, and found it interesting to note how laughter in animals may identify new molecules to alleviate depression, disorders of excessive exuberance (such as mania and ADHD), addictive urges, and mood imbalances.

Quoting ancient authors, James Young Thomson Greig writes that "laughter is not believed to begin in a child until the child is forty days old."

According to Robert Provine,

Laughter is a mechanism everyone has; laughter is a part of universal human vocabulary. People say that there are thousands of languages, hundreds of thousands of dialects, but everyone speaks laughter in pretty much the same way.

Everyone can laugh. Babies have the ability to laugh before they ever speak. Children who are born blind and deaf still retain the ability to laugh. Even apes have a form of "pant-pant-pant" laughter. That's true! I have observed this phenomenon in the jungles of Brunei, when we took a boat trip with other tourists to view the monkeys leaping from tree to tree and creating the "pant-pant-pant laughter." Indeed, it was an amazingly entertaining sight that we caught on our video cameras.

Provine argues that "laughter is a primitive and an unconscious vocalization." And it means if you laugh more than others, it is probably genetic. This is backed up by the story of the "giggle twins," described in this story:

> *Two exceptionally happy twins were separated at birth and not reunited forty years later. Provine reports that until they met each other, neither of these exceptionally happy ladies had known anyone who laughed as much as each did. They were both reared by different sets of adoptive parents whom they described as "undemonstrative and dour." Provine concluded that "the twins inherited some aspects of their laugh and sound and pattern, readiness to laugh, and perhaps, even taste in humor."*

Gender Differences in Laughter

Men and women take jokes differently. A study shows that ten men and ten women all watched ten cartoons and rated them as funny or not funny, and if funny how funny on a scale of one to ten. While doing this, their brains were all scanned using functional magnetic resonance imaging (FMRI). Men and women for the most part agreed on which cartoons were funny. However, their brains handled humor differently. Women's brains showed more activity in certain areas, including the nucleus accumbens. When women viewed cartoons that they did not find humorous, their nucleus accumbens had a "hohum response."

The differences between men and women, from time immemorial, have always been highlighted in numerous different ways: psychologically, physically, mentally, socially, and sometimes even spiritually.

Laughter and a Sense of Well-being

They say that when you laugh, it boosts the serotonin level in your brain, and that makes you happy and improves your sense of well-being. A lot of people say they experience this effect, based upon their funny experiences in life. Indeed, it is very true! Having happy thoughts relates directly to your sense of well-being.

In fact, some claim that lack of serotonin in the brain causes depression. Conversely, an increase of serotonin in the brain caused simply by laughing can alleviate depression and other issues related to mental health.

I am a person who turns on the television only when I know there is something extraordinary to watch or listen to. And when I watch television, usually before dinner, I want to relax and somehow get updated on what's happening around me and around the world that we live in. But one thing I love to watch is high-caliber comedy shows, ones that really make me laugh or chuckle!

Laughing is fun! I love to laugh when the occasion calls for it. Laughing can do you no harm. It's good for your health and brightens your life. Happy people know how to laugh. Some people need laughter to get them well.

Do you laugh? How does laughing affect you? How do you feel during or after laughing? Do you feel good? Do you think laughter should be a part of your everyday life? Or do you even think it is important to make laughter a part of your life?

Five Jokes that Will Make You Laugh

1. Best "Out-of-Office" Automatic Email Replies

- I am currently out at a job interview and will reply to you if I fail to get the position. Be prepared for my mood.

- You are receiving this automatic notification because I am out of the office. If I was in, chances are you wouldn't have received anything at all.

- Sorry I have missed you, but I am at the doctor's having my brain and heart removed so I can be promoted to our management team.

- I will be unable to delete all the unread, worthless emails you send me until I return from vacation. Please be patient and your mail will be deleted in the order it was received.

- Thank you for your email. Your credit card has been charged $5.99 for the first ten words and $1.99 for each additional word in your message.

- The email server is unable to verify your server connection and is unable to deliver this message. Please restart your computer and try sending again. (The beauty of this is that when you return, you can see how many in-duh-viduals did this over and over.)

- Thank you for your message, which has been added to a queuing system. You are currently in 352nd place and can expect to receive a reply in approximately nineteen weeks.

- Hi, I'm thinking about what you've just sent me. Please wait by your PC for my response.
- I've run away to join a different circus.
- I will be out of the office for the next two weeks for medical reasons. When I return, please refer to me as "Loretta" instead of "Bob."

2. An Aussie Lad

A young Aussie lad moved to London and went to Harrods looking for a job. The manager asked, "Do you have any sales experience?"

The young man answered, "Yeah, I was a salesman back home." The manager liked the Aussie, so he gave him the job.

His first day on the job was challenging and busy, but he got through it. After the store was locked up, the manager came down and asked, "Okay, so how many sales did you make today?"

The Aussie said, "One."

The manager groaned and continued, "Just one? Our sales people average twenty or thirty sales a day. How much was the sale for?

"£101,237.64."

The manager choked and exclaimed, "£101,237.64? What the hell did you sell him?"

"Well, first I sold him a snorkel, then some flippers, and then I sold him a new wetsuit. Then I asked him where he was going snorkeling, and he said down at the coast, so I told him he would need a boat, so we went down to the boat department and I sold him that twin-engined Power Cat. Then he said he didn't think his Honda Civic would pull it, so I took him down to car sales and I sold him the 4x4 Suzuki".

The manager, incredulous, said, "You mean to tell me, a guy came in here to buy a snorkel and you sold him a boat and 4x4?"

"No, no, no. He came in here to buy a box of tampons for his lady friend, and I said, 'Well, since your weekend's mucked up, you might as well go snorkeling.'"

3. New Super Market Sounds (LOL)

The new supermarket near our house has an automatic water mist to keep the produce fresh. Just before it goes on, you hear the sound of distant thunder and the smell of fresh rain. The produce department features the smell of fresh-buttered corn. When you approach the milk cases, you hear cows mooing and experience the scent of fresh hay. When you approach the egg case, you hear hens cluck and cackle and the air is filled with the pleasing aroma of bacon and eggs frying. I don't buy toilet paper there any more.

4. "Ticket, please."

Three Microsoft engineers and three Apple employees are traveling by train to a computer conference. At the station, the three Microsoft engineers each buy tickets and watch as the three Apple employees buy only a single ticket.

"How are three people going to travel on only one ticket?" asks a Microsoft engineer.

"Watch and you'll see," answers the Apple employee.

They all board the train. The Microsoft engineers take their respective seats, but all three Apple employees cram into a restroom and close the door behind them. Shortly after the train has departed, the conductor comes around collecting tickets. He knocks on the restroom door and says, "Ticket, please." The door opens just a crack and a single arm emerges with a ticket in hand. The conductor takes the ticket and moves on.

The Microsoft engineers saw this and agreed it was quite a clever idea. So after the conference, the Microsoft engineers decide to do the same on the return trip and save some money. When they get to the station, they buy a single ticket for the return trip. To their astonishment, the Apple employees don't buy any ticket, at all.

"How are you going to travel without a ticket?" asks one perplexed Microsoft engineer.

"Watch and you'll see," answers an Apple employee.

When they board the train, the three Microsoft engineers cram into a restroom and the three Apple employees cram into another one nearby. The train departs. Shortly afterward, one of the Apple employees leaves his restroom and walks over to the restroom where the Microsoft engineers are hiding. He knocks on the door and says, "Ticket, please."

5. Health Question and Answer Session

Q: I've heard that cardiovascular exercise can prolong life. Is this true?

A: Your heart is only good for so many beats, and that's it. Don't waste them on exercise. Everything wears out eventually. Speeding up your heart will not make you live longer; that's like saying you can extend the life of your car by driving it faster. Want to live longer? Take a nap.

Q: Should I cut down on meat and eat more fruits and vegetables?

A: You must grasp logistical efficiencies. What does a cow eat? Hay and corn. And what are these? Vegetables. So a steak is nothing more than an efficient mechanism of delivering vegetables to your system. Need grain? Eat chicken. Beef is also a good source of field grass (green leafy vegetable). And a pork chop can give you 100 percent of your recommended daily allowance of vegetable products.

Q: Should I reduce my alcohol intake?

A: No, not at all. Wine is made from fruit. Brandy is distilled wine, that means they take the water out of the fruity bit so you get even more of the goodness that way. Beer is also made out of grain. Bottoms up!

Q: How can I calculate my body/fat ratio?

A: Well, if you have a body and you have fat, your ratio is one to one. If you have two bodies, your ratio is two to one, etc.

Q: What are some of the advantages of participating in a regular exercise program?

A: Can't think of a single one, sorry. My philosophy is: No pain? Good!

Q: Aren't fried foods bad for you?

A: You're not listening. Foods are fried these days in vegetable oil. In fact, they're permeated in it. How could getting more vegetables be bad for you?

Q: Will sit-ups help prevent me from getting a little soft around the middle?

A: Definitely not! When you exercise a muscle, it gets bigger. You should only be doing sit-ups if you want a bigger stomach.

Q: Is chocolate bad for me?

A: Are you crazy? Hello cocoa beans! Another vegetable. It's the best feel-good food around!

Q: Is swimming good for your figure?

A: If swimming is good for your figure, explain whales to me.

Q: Is getting in shape important for my lifestyle?

A: Hey! 'Round' is a shape!

Well, I hope this has cleared up any misconceptions you may have had about food and diets.

And remember: "Life should not be a journey to the grave with the intention of arriving safely in an attractive and well preserved body, but rather to skid in sideways, Chardonnay in one hand, chocolate in the other, body thoroughly used up, totally worn out, and screaming, "Woo hoo, what a ride!"

Reader Exercise

A. Enumerate five ways to bring laughter into your everyday life

1. _____

2. _____

3. _____

4. _____

5. _____

B. List five things that make you laugh

1. _____

2. _____

3. _____

4. _____

5. _____

Laugh more! It can only do you good!

Whatever differences exist between men and women, it is crucial to remember the following thoughts:

LIVE well.

LAUGH often.

LOVE with all of your heart.

LOVE well; LAUGH often; LOVE with all of your heart.

Let there be more laughter in your living.

chapter 7

Power Word Number Seven:

Be Happy!

Therefore, be at peace with God, whatever you conceive Him to be; and whatever your labors and aspirations, in the noisy confusion of life, keep peace with your soul. With all its shams, drudgery and broken dreams, it is still a beautiful world. Be cheerful. Strive to be happy.

—MAX EHRMANN, *DESIDERATA*

Happiness, some would argue, is a state of mind. It is something seated deep in the heart and in the mind. It comes from within, not from without. It is the spring of joy that comes gushing forth in its true beauty.

Sometimes, perhaps numerous times, people destroy their present happiness by dwelling on a distant misery, which may never come at all. You may well be familiar with the Biblical verse that warns you not to borrow tomorrow's troubles today: "Therefore do not worry about tomorrow, for tomorrow will worry about itself. Each day has enough trouble of its own" (Matt. 6:34).

Happiness and the Law of Attraction

People whose minds are positive, recharged, optimistic, enthusiastic, and happy will tell you that every substantial grief has twenty shadows, and most of the shadows are of your own making. That's true in many ways! Why is it so? It is because it is all in your mind. That's why you are discouraged from giving life to your fears, because your fears might just become reality. What you conceive and believe, you achieve. That's the Law of Attraction in motion.

When you think happy and positive thoughts, you achieve positive and happy outcomes. When you think negative thoughts, you get negative results. You create what you think, and if your mind is plagued with lots of negative thoughts, you reap negative results. It always goes back to the Law of Attraction: "What you conceive and perceive, you achieve."

Happiness and Change

Friedrich von Schiller, the German author, dramatist, poet, and author of *William Tell*, has left in me a very significant and powerful thought about happiness. It is a short but unforgettable statement which, indeed,

I have never forgotten. The statement is taken from *William Tell,* so let me just give you a very brief historical background about the character William Tell.

History tells us that William Tell was the legendary Swiss hero who lived in the fourteenth century, a Swiss version of Robin Hood. Tell symbolized the struggle for political and individual freedom. Schiller's play is an action adventure set in the fourteenth century during the hostile Austrian occupation of Switzerland. Some, however, have questioned whether he really existed. Was he just a legend?

I remember the trip I made to Switzerland with my husband in 2005. Strolling in the beautiful and historic town of Altdorf in Switzerland, we saw the tall and majestic monument of William Tell. Since it was a historical emblem, I was excited to a pose in front of the monument, and I asked my husband to take my photo with the monument behind me. But what's so exciting or meaningful, you might ask, about having a photo taken at William Tell's monument? I'll tell you why, because I wanted to highlight what the author of *William Tell*'s said of happiness. Schiller wrote:

Happy is he who learns to bear what he cannot change.

To me, this gives you strength of mind and spirit and gives you the courage and vigor to meet challenging circumstances as you face them and tackle them each day of your life. Schiller's thought on happiness reminds me of the well-known prayer written by Reinhold Niebuhr:

God grant me the serenity to accept the things I cannot change; the courage to change the things I can, and the wisdom to know the difference.

Happy is he who learns to bear what he can not change.

- JOHANN CRISTOPH FREDRICH VON SCHILLER

AUTHOR, *WILHELM TELL*

(MONUMENT OF WILHELM TELL IN SWITZERLAND)

Someone has said that you have to be open to your happiness and sadness as they arise. Take note of the encouraging words of Thomas St. Clair:

> *Strong, pure, and happy thoughts build up the body in vigor and grace. Calmness of mind is one of the beautiful jewels of wisdom.*

Three Critical Keys to Happiness: Communication, Relationships, and Empathy

Communication and relationships with others are two of the critical keys to happiness. Hence, they say, "Walk in another's moccasins or shoes." So, there is nothing like "walking in another's moccasins" before you even think of speaking your mind. This is what we call empathy—"feeling with" the other person—another of the keys to happiness.

Empathy is the process of trying to understand the other person's point of view, as if you were that person.

One of the ways to begin to practice empathy is to be more open and sensitive to the needs and differences of others. We are told that successful individuals look at relatives rather than absolutes.

We are, therefore, forewarned: the prelude to empathy is the realization that each human being on earth is a person with equal rights to fulfill his or her own potential in life. It means understanding that skin color, birthplace, political beliefs, sex, financial status, and intelligence are not the true measures worth or happiness.

The key to communication is accepting the fact that every human being is a distinctly unique individual and thinking how good that is. No two people are alike, not even identical twins.

In this connection, God is not an idea or a definition that we have committed to memory. He is a presence that we experience in our hearts.

I want to share with you some fifteen steps you can take to become happy and also seventeen tips that I discovered on WikiHow.com while I was doing some online research.

Fifteen Steps on How to Be Happy:

Step 1:   Change your thought process.

Step 2:   See the world for what it really is.

Step 3:   Lighten up.

Step 4:   Be yourself.

Step 5:   Make a scheduled time every day for relaxation.

Step 6:   Get a job you love.

Step 7:   Develop a strong relationship with your family.

Step 8:   Choose the right companion.

Step 9:   Choose your friends carefully.

Step 10:   Do what you can for those less fortunate than yourself.

Step 11:   Wish the best for others and mean it.

Step 12:   Keep learning.

Step 13:   Set goals.

Step 14:   Be healthy.

Step 15:   Strive for long-term goals rather than short-term satisfaction.

Seventeen Happiness Tips

Tip 1:   Learn the techniques of self-assertion. If you have problems, get your feelings and opinions out instead of using anger or bottling them up inside you.

Tip 2:   Take up spiritual practice. Research has proven that people detached from the problems of this life are calmer, happier, and more contented. Turning to a higher being other than yourself and this world and its problems gives you a sense of inner peace.

Tip 3:   Try to make someone else happy and you will feel happy.

Tip 4:   Use a simple mental strategy for life. Think about something good that happened to you, and then explore how this contributed to that good feeling and feeling happy about yourself.

Tip 5:   Listen to music that will make you feel good. When you wake up, put on some uplifting music.

Tip 6:   Be honest with yourself. Ask yourself if there's something that is keeping you from being happy— perhaps an addiction, an insecurity, or something else.

Tip 7:   Stop stressing about money or about things out of your control.

Tip 8:   Get plenty of sleep every night.

Tip 9:   When you receive a compliment from others, accept it and say thank you.

Tip 10: Get healthy or stay healthy by eating right and exercising.

Tip 11:   Learn to be happy with what you already have. Never ever compare your life with that of others.

Tip 12:   Pay your bills on time, and be in the habit of keeping an orderly home. Treat yourself to something special once in a while, not because you need it, but just because you want it.

Tip 13:   Care for and love a pet once you reach your goals. If you have the time, energy, and stability to take the responsibility of caring for a pet, you might consider this. (Don't rush into this or adopt a pet for the wrong reasons! This is a long-term commitment but also a great way to share your happiness.)

Tip 14:   Make new friends and talk to them about your problems.

Tip 15:   Find a boyfriend or girlfriend and fall in love.

Tip 16:   Get out of your house and hang out with friends.

Tip 17:   Even in the most terrible times, do not turn to alcohol or drugs.

Three Warnings about Happiness

Warning 1: If you can't be happy from within and be satisfied with what you have or who you are, then you will never be truly happy with anyone else.

Warning 2: You can only buy temporary happiness. True and lasting happiness must come from within.

Warning 3: Do not spend your money only for necessities. Money is only a tool to acquire the things you need or want in life. Do not love the tool or become a slave to it. Occasionally, you should treat yourself and others to something special to enjoy the fruits of your labor.

Og Mandino's Five Great Laws of Success and Happiness

I want to share with you Og Mandino's Five Great Laws of Success and Happiness. His noble, time-tested ideas on success and happiness can guide you on your own path to success and happiness when you implement them in your everyday life.

Law 1:   Count your blessings.

Law 2:   Proclaim your rarity.

Law 3:   Go another mile!

Law 4:   Use wisely your power of choice.

Law 5:   Do all things with love—love for yourself and love for others.

Do everything possible on your part to live in peace with everybody. (Rom. 12:18)

In moral philosophy:

That action is best which procures the greatest happiness for the greatest number.

Keep your mindset in peace, joy and victory.
Be Happy!

Happy people will go out and enjoy life.

Happiness waits outside.

Rediscover your own backyard or your front porch.

Enjoy the landscape.

Watch the clouds pass by –

Nature is right there alongside you.

Epilogue

You are your own life strategist.

Revolutionize your life and take it to the next level by simply implementing the seven power words.

The goal of this book, *The 7 Power Words: A Guide to a Truly Happy and Meaningful Life,* is to give you an unbelievable opportunity to acquire the knowledge of the seven power words that can assist you in developing the skills and strategies you need to live an enjoyable, happy, and meaningful life!

Knowing, learning and implementing *The 7 Power Words* everyday will fill your life with *real* happiness and meaning and how to live your life to the fullest.

Putting these power words into action will replace your sense of aimless dissatisfaction in your life with a sense of purpose. The wealth of information that you gather from the *7 Power Words* could save you years of frustration and heartache.

One happiness tip is to get plenty of sleep.

Happiness is nurturing the environment.

Happiness is rediscovering your own back-yard on your front porch.

What happens outwardly in your life sometimes is not as important as what happens inside of you. Therefore, you will learn how to abandon unhappiness and achieve a true lasting happiness. In the process, you will discover the "real you" and unleash the joy within. In James 1:12 in the Bible, it says:

> *Blessed is the man who perseveres under trial, because when*
> *he has stood the test, he will receive the crown of life that*
> *God has promised to those who love him.*

The tips on right mental attitude will encourage you to build your spiritual life. They will also help strengthen you and help you face the daily challenges you encounter in your life. And they will direct you towards a successful life. Hence, they give you the opportunity to reclaim the daily joy of living a meaningful life.

The 7 Power Words: A Guide to a Truly Happy and Meaningful Life teaches you how to sharpen your outlook and excel both at work and at home and to make the best use of your time and learn how to relax and avoid harmful stress.

Overall, the *7 Power Words* will give you the strategies to properly express your character and individuality. By implementing these seven powerful words—Live, Love, Think, Learn, Give, Laugh, and Be Happy—in positive ways, you will be guided to live a truly happy and meaningful life with purpose.

> *There is no growth without change, no change without fear*
> *or loss, and no loss without pain. Nothing is inevitable*
> *until it happens.*

The principle of human dignity, the basic concept in the United States Declaration of Independence, upholds this principle. It is written:

> *We hold these truths to be self-evident: that all men are created equal and endowed by their Creator with certain inalienable rights, that among these are life, liberty and the pursuit of happiness.*

—DECLARATION OF HUMAN RIGHTS

Put your life on overdrive and step

up the next level of your life.

—Letty Rulloda Stevens Vendramini

ASPIRE TO REACH YOUR POTENTIAL!

Happiness is nature right there alongside you.

Appendix

The ABCs of Happiness

A spire to reach your potential.

B elieve in yourself.

C reate a good life.

D ream of what you may become.

E xercise frequently.

F orgive honest mistakes.

G lorify the creative spirit.

H umor yourself and others.

I magine great things.

J oyfully live each day.

K indly help others.

L ove one another.

M editate daily.

N urture the environment.

O rganize for harmonious action.

P raise performance well done.

Q uestion most things.

R egulate your behavior.

S mile often.

T hink rationally.

U nderstand yourself.

V alue life.

W ork for the common good.

X -ray and carefully examine problems.

Y earn to improve.

Z estfully pursue happiness.

—ROBERT VALETT, FROM *PRESCRIPTIONS OF HAPPINESS*

> "Be happy where you are."
>
> "Bloom where you are planted."

Promise Yourself

To be so strong, so that nothing can disturb your peace of mind.

To talk health, happiness, and prosperity to every person you meet.

To make all your friends feel that there is something in them.

To look at the sunny side of everything and make your optimism

come true.

To think only of the best, to work only for the best, and to expect
only the best of others as you are about your own.

To forget the mistakes of the past, and to press on to the greater
achievements of the future.

To wear a cheerful countenance at all times, and give every living
creature you meet a smile.

To give so much time to the improvement of yourself that you have
no time to criticize others.

To be too large to worry, too noble for anger, too strong for fear,
and too happy to permit the presence of trouble.

Introduction to Father Bob Garon

I think I feel the same sentiments as Father Bob Garon, who, when he
finds an inspirational piece of reading, shares it with everyone he knows.
The following reading, he says, is a prayer that he read from Og Mandino
that touched him deeply and one that he found beautiful and practical. I
have kept this beautiful prayer for more than two decades, ever since my
older sister mailed it to me from the United States when I was grieving
the loss of my first husband.

This prayer has given me strength, inner peace, direction, and guidance
in my life, especially when I most needed it, and it continues to guide me
in my everyday life. I kept this prayer safe in one of my files, and I still
use it as one of my daily prayers.

I want to share this reading with you, too. Father Garon said that
it is "A Meditation of Life and Our Response to It." Learn from the

wisdom of Og Mandino's prayer and savor the powerful words that will help you live the life you've always wanted—a life of peace, fulfillment, joy, success, health, wealth, and true happiness. Father Garon suggested you to clip it out and put it somewhere where you can uses it in your daily prayers.

A Meditation on Life and Your Response to It

God, thank you for this day.

I know I have not accomplished as yet all you expect of me, and if that is your reason for bathing me in the fresh dew of another dawn, I am most grateful.

I am prepared, at last, to make you proud of me. I will forget yesterday, with all its trials and tribulations, aggravations and setbacks, angers and frustrations. The past is already a dream from which I can neither retrieve a single word nor erase any foolish deeds.

I will not fret the future. My success and happiness does not depend on straining to see what lurks dimly on the horizon but to do, this day, what lies clearly at hand.

I will treasure this day, for it is all I have. I know that its trials and rushing hours cannot be accumulated or stored, like precious grain, for future use.

I will live as all good actors do when they are on stage—only in the moment. I cannot perform at my best today by regretting my precious grain, for future use.

I will embrace today's difficult tasks, take off my coat, and make dust in the world. I will remember that the busier I am, the less harm that I am apt to suffer. The tastier will be my food, the sweeter my sleep, and the better satisfied I will be with my place in the world.

I will free myself today of slavery of the clock and calendar. Although I will plan this day to conserve my steps and energy, I will begin to measure my life in deed, in thoughts, not seasons; in feelings, not figures on a dial.

I will remain aware of how little it takes. Never will I pursue happiness, for it is not a goal, just a by-product, and there is no happiness in giving or getting, only in giving.

I will run from no danger I might encounter today, because I am certain that nothing will happen to me that I am not equipped to handle with your help. Just as any gem is polished by friction, I am certain to become more valuable through this day's adversities, and if you close one door, you always open another for me.

I will live this day as if it were Christmas. I will be a giver of gifts and deliver my enemies the gift of forgiveness; my opponents, tolerance; my friends, a smile; my children, a good example; and every gift will be wrapped with unconditional love.

I will waste not even a precious second today in anger or hate or jealousy or selfishness. I know that the seeds I sow I will harvest, because every action, good or bad, is always followed by an equal reaction. I will only plant good seeds today.

—FR. BOB GARON, INSPIRED BY OG MANDINO

Echoes of My Mind: A Soliloquy on Life

by Letty R. Stevens (1997)

In moments when solitude and tranquility invade me, it often leaves me musing about LIFE. What is this thing called life? When people have troubles they say: "That's life!" "So is life!" "Life is not a bed of roses." "Live life to the fullest!" "Take one day at a time." But what do these statements really mean?

Do we really understand them at all?

Do we really understand what life is all about?

Are we meant to understand life or to live it?

Do we fully know how to live life and give meaning to it?

But if we do, why the chaos in the world?

Why the uncertainty creeping in individual lives?

Why the panic? The confusion? The stress? The turmoil?

Why is the world in a mess? Why?

For a moment I pause …, my lingering thoughts just wandering around.

Is there anyone to blame? But who is to blame?

Is there any answer to all the chaos? But what is the answer?

Is there anything we can do? But what shall we do?

Perhaps a lot begins with the SELF:

A maintenance of our sterling characters—never violating the direction of our conscience; never say or do anything unless you have accurate information; have confidence in yourself! Never forget that the Almighty God sees and knows everything that you say, do, or think and He is keeping a record of these things. Aim to please God in everything that you do.

Don't look for success too quickly or too certainly.

Work hard! Don't invest today and expect to get your investment with interest back tomorrow.

Refuse to become discouraged or defeated—

Failure is never important if it is not final.

Try to develop and cultivate seriousness of purpose, simplicity of life, courage, and strength.

Undertake your work in the reverential respect of God which is the beginning of all wisdom.

Ground your work on righteousness of life, which is the only sure, sound, and safe foundation.

If you begin life in this spirit, there will be little danger of complete and final failure.

Be conscientious about your progress but not worrisome, although some worries are stimulating and help us to get things done.

Regardless of how many pressing things are upon you, do only one thing at a time.

Put aside all anxiety; keep your eyes and ears open.

Do that which is nearest at hand and do it as well as you can.

Never build your reputation at another's expense.

Anything less than the utmost development of your capacities is a frightful mistake, an inexcusable blunder, a waste of God's gifts.

We cannot arrive at perfection, but that does not relieve us of the obligation and responsibility of trying to do our best. Be as Godlike (in everything) as imperfect creatures can be.

> Your lives have been years of self-discovery, insight, wonder, and excitement: You now can say to yourselves that you can get as much as you have put in it.

> For people who want to make their own way ahead, you can have a lasting effect on your LIFE—that is, if you want to work on it.

> What your future is going to be depends largely on what you perceive and dream it to be. Find out what your REAL DREAMS are—then strive, stretch, and reach out for them. Grow as much as your horizon allows. Everything you do is somehow designed to achieving your fulfillment and happiness. But this is NOT ALL.

> ALL of these goals, all of these ideas, all of these concerns touch upon your lives, shape your future, and deeply influence your present moment.

Keep in mind:

When the going gets tough, let the tough get going.

REAL LIFE and real living belong to men and women who know what they want and want what they know.

LUCK HAS NO PLACE WHEN SURVIVAL IS AT STAKE. Make your way—touch and reach life. Someone has said:

> *"Others have built your past;*
> *you build your future."*

LIVE! Start now; let yourself be! Don't just stand there. GET STARTED!

Set out your goal for yourself, for "the beginning is just the half thing."

Living is a responsibility. Life is searching. Let's seek with the desire to know more, and find with the desire to seek more.

As beloved sons and daughters of the Universe, never shame yourselves or your Mother!

("Echoes of My Mind: A Soliloquy on Life" by Letty R. Stevens has been published in the *Philippine Community Herald Newspaper* (PCHN), a monthly publication based in Sydney and distributed Australia-wide.)

Thank you, stay happy and God bless you all!

LETTY R. STEVENS VENDRAMINI

Live YOUR life to the Fullest!

Empower YOURSELF with the 7 Life-Transforming and Empowering Power Words to guide you to a truly happy and meaningful life!

To achieve your dreams, be confident, passionate, enthusiastic, resilient, and wise with the skills, strategies and guides you have learned in this book, *The 7 Power Words: A Guide to a Truly Happy and Meaningful Life.* Whatever you conceive in your mind and believe, you can achieve, so be fearless in your actions towards achieving your goals and dreams.

The poem below, which I wrote under the name Letty R. Stevens, appeared in 1997 in the book *Voices Diverse: A Collection* (page 9), published by the Multicultural Writers Association of Queensland (Australia), of which I was a member, and printed in Australia by Fast Books, Sydney.

This poem was dedicated to my son, Peter, who was then fourteen years old.

Fear Not

May we all be like the sturdy tree,
  strongly rooted and standing firm
    ever ready to accept whatever sunshine
    and rain life may bring.

  As long as the trunk is firm,
    Worry not
  over the branches swaying in the wind.

In life ...,
    If you wish to be great,
      Fear not the storms of life.
    If you wish to be rich,
      Fear not the blinding heat.
    If you wish to be renowned,
      Fear not the darkest night.
    If you wish to be loved,
      Fear not the stormy path.

  Fear not, young man—
      Above, there is your goal;
      Above, there is your guiding star;
      Above, there is your loving God.

Fear not, young man ..., fear not!
  Like the sturdy tree,
    sail on your ship
      with the tides of life.

—LETTY R. STEVENS

QUEENSLAND AUSTRALIA, 1997

> Whatever you can do
>
> or dream you can,
>
> begin it.
>
> Boldness has genius,
>
> magic, and power in it.
>
> Begin it now.
>
> —GOETHE

The Next Stage

Speaking Engagements

- To request Letty R. Vendramini to speak at your next event and learn more about her other information products and services, please visit her website…

  www.LettyVendramini.com

- Letty is an International Speaker, an Alumnus of the John Childers' Million Dollar International Speaker Training.

- As a professional educator, she had ten years experience teaching Public Speaking and Argumentation and Debate at the tertiary level.

- She is regularly invited as Master of Ceremonies in small and big social, organizational, community, and state events, hosting from 250 to 3000 guests.

- Letty speaks also as Motivational Speaker at global conferences, peak body organizations, at the Australian-Filipino Chamber of Commerce, other professional and social organizations, and clubs.

FREE eBook Bonus

"SPECIAL Happiness Report"

When you buy a copy of the book *7 Power Words: A Guide To A Truly Happy And Meaningful Life*, you can download the FREE eBook by going to this link:

http://www.LettyVendramini.com/bonusreport/

Some of the features of the *SPECIAL Happiness Report* worth reading and knowing include:

- The differences between what happiness Is and what happiness is NOT;
- How to "Be Thyself";
- The features of unhappiness to avoid;

- How to move towards happiness;
- Experiencing full happiness
- And many more

"Thank you so much" for purchasing a copy of my book, *The 7 Power Words: A Guide To A Truly Happy And Meaningful Life.* I sincerely hope that the power words and strategies presented and discussed in this book will help anyone in finding and achieving his/her everyday happiness, and true happiness and meaning in life.

To your Happiness and Success! God bless you!

Sincerely yours

Letty R. Vendramini

Bibliography

Covey, Stephen R. *The Seven Habits of Highly Effective People*. New
    York: Simon and Schuster, 1990.

Greig, John Young Thomson. *The Psychology of Laughter and Comedy*.
    London: George Allen and Unwin, 1923.

Hayward, Susan. *A Guide for the Advanced Soul*. Avalon, NSW,
    Australia: In Tune Books, 1984.

The Holy Bible. New International Version. Grand Rapids, MI:
    Zondervan, 1984.

Mandino, Og. *Three Volumes in One: The Greatest Salesman in the World,*
    The Greatest Secret in The World, The Greatest Miracle in the World.
    New York: Bonanza Books, 1981.

Moore, Brooke Noel, and Richard Parker. *Critical Thinking*, 8th ed.
    New York: McGraw-Hill, 2005.

Osteen, Joel. *Your Best Life NOW: Seven Steps to Living Your Potential*.
    New York: Warner Faith Book Co., 2004.

Purnell, Dick. *Building a Relationship That Lasts*. San Bernardino, CA:
    Here's Life Publishers, 1998.

Schuller, Robert H. *Tough Times Never Last But Tough People Do.* New York: Bantam Books, 1983.

Savelle, Jerry. *A Right Mental Attitude: The Doorway to a Successful Life.* Tulsa, OK: Harrison House, 1980.

Waitley, Denis. *Seeds of Greatness: The Ten Best-Kept Secrets of Total Success.* London: Cedar Books, 1993.

Warren, Rick. *The Purpose-Driven Life.* Grand Rapids, MI: Zondervan, 2002.

Wimbrey, Johnny D. *From the Hood to Doing Good.* Dallas, Texas: Brown Books Publishing, 2003.

About the Author

Letty R. Vendramini

Letty R. Vendramini is an international speaker, author, personal and happiness coach, Internet infopreneur, educator, philosopher, newspaper columnist, reporter/correspondent, editor, writer, and EzineArticles.com "expert author." Her niche market is in Personal Development/Self/Help. Her diverse professional backgrounds are philosophy, English, social work, and counseling. Letty's teaching career in the tertiary level spans twelve years, both in the Philippines and in Australia. She also worked in Australia as a private practitioner in social work and counseling and a social worker in a government hospital and a peak-body organization of 161 ethnicities from all over the world.

She taught subjects in philosophy, English grammar and composition, research and thesis writing, essay and essay writing, literature, public speaking, argumentation and debate, general psychology, and business ethics.

Letty is the founder and creator of BestSecretsToHappiness.com and publisher and editor of the online "Happiness Tips Newsletter." She is the author of the *SPECIAL Happiness Report* and author of *The 7 Power Words: A Guide to a Truly Happy and Meaningful Life.*

In Queensland, Australia, Letty has largely contributed and played major roles in projects in conjunction with the Philippine Embassy in Australia and the Philippine Consulate in Brisbane for the Filipino community and the Australian mainstream society. Likewise, she has been a vital force in the Filipino Community Council of Queensland (FCCQ, Inc.), the peak body organization of Filipino organizations in the State of Queensland where she held key positions in the Executive Committee as Secretary, Treasurer, Media Officer, Editor of the Souvenir Programs and Newsletters. She was a regular appointee as Master of Ceremonies in big community annual celebrations and fundraising events at various organizations.

Visit: www.BestSecretsToHappiness.com/bonusreport/

Million Dollar International Speaker

Founder/Creator – *Best Secrets To Happiness*

Author: The 7 Power Words…

Author: *SPECIAL Happiness Report*

Publisher:/Editor: 'Happiness Tips Newsletter'

Personal & Happiness Coach

Ezine Articles.com "Expert Author"

URL: http://www.BestSecretsToHappiness.com/

URL: http://www.BestSecretsToHappiness.com/blog/

URL: http://www.7PowerWords.com/

URL: http://vendramini.successuniversity.com/

P.O.Box 949, Capalaba, QLD, Australia 4157

BUY A SHARE OF THE FUTURE IN YOUR COMMUNITY

These certificates make great holiday, graduation and birthday gifts that can be personalized with the recipient's name. The cost of one S.H.A.R.E. or one square foot is $54.17. The personalized certificate is suitable for framing and will state the number of shares purchased and the amount of each share, as well as the recipient's name. The home that you participate in "building" will last for many years and will continue to grow in value.

Here is a sample SHARE certificate:

YES, I WOULD LIKE TO HELP!

*I support the work that Habitat for Humanity does and I want to be part of the excitement! As a donor, I will receive periodic updates on your construction activities but, more importantly, I know my gift will help a family in our community realize the dream of homeownership. **I would like to SHARE in your efforts against substandard housing in my community!** (Please print below)*

PLEASE SEND ME _____ SHARES at $54.17 EACH = $ $_____

In Honor Of: _____

Occasion: (Circle One)   HOLIDAY   BIRTHDAY   ANNIVERSARY

     OTHER: _____

Address of Recipient: _____

Gift From: _____ *Donor Address:* _____

Donor Email: _____

I AM ENCLOSING A CHECK FOR $ $_____ PAYABLE TO HABITAT FOR HUMANITY <u>OR</u> PLEASE CHARGE MY VISA OR MASTERCARD *(CIRCLE ONE)*

Card Number _____ Expiration Date: _____

Name as it appears on Credit Card _____ Charge Amount $ _____

Signature _____

Billing Address _____

Telephone # Day _____ Eve _____

PLEASE NOTE: Your contribution is tax-deductible to the fullest extent allowed by law.
Habitat for Humanity • P.O. Box 1443 • Newport News, VA 23601 • 757-596-5553
www.HelpHabitatforHumanity.org